THE  SERIES

BATTLESHIP ARIZONA'S
MARINES AT WAR

MAKING THE ULTIMATE SACRIFICE, DECEMBER 7, 1941

DICK CAMP

ZENITH
PRESS

First published in 2006 by Zenith Press, an imprint of MBI Publishing Company, Galtier Plaza, Suite 200, 380 Jackson Street, St. Paul, MN 55101-3885 USA

Zenith Press titles are also available at discounts in bulk quantity for industrial or sales-promotional use. For details write to Special Sales Manager at MBI Publishing Company, Galtier Plaza, Suite 200, 380 Jackson Street, St. Paul, MN 55101-3885 USA.

On the cover: Formal *Arizona* Marine detachment photo, circa 1920. *History Division, USMC*

Frontispiece: A painting based on a 1916 photograph of the *USS Arizona's* sister ship, the *Pennsylvania*, in New York's East River with the Brooklyn Bridge in the background. *Author's collection*

Title page: *Arizona* at sea. President Hoover's flag flies from the mainmast. *National Archives 80-G-461035*

About the author: Dick Camp is a retired Marine Corps colonel and the author of *Lima-6*, his memoir as a Marine infantry company commander at Khe Sanh, which has been described as "an outstanding true story. A tremendous book recounting . . . the challenges of leading [young] Marines in war time." He is also the author of *Leatherneck Legends: Conversations with the Marine Corps' Old Breed*. Over his twenty-six-year career, he served with two of the five legends covered in that book. Colonel Camp is deputy directory of the History Division of the Marine Corps University at Quantico, Virginia.

Library of Congress Cataloging-in-Publication Data

Camp, Richard D.
Battleship Arizona's Marines at war : making the ultimate sacrifice, December 7, 1941 / Dick Camp.
    p. cm.
Includes bibliographical references and index.
ISBN-13: 978-0-7603-2717-3 (softbound)
ISBN-10: 0-7603-2717-3 (softbound)
1. Arizona (Battleship) 2. United States. Marine Corps. Marine Detachment Arizona. 3. Pearl Harbor (Hawaii), Attack on, 1941. I. Title.
D774.A67C36 2006
940.54'26693--dc22
                                    2006014798

Editor: Scott Pearson
Designer: Christopher Fayers

Printed in China

CONTENTS

PROLOGUE   **AND THE BAND PLAYED ON**   6

CHAPTER ONE   **MARINE DETACHMENT ARIZONA**   8

CHAPTER TWO   **FROM REVOLUTION TO PEARL HARBOR**   24

CHAPTER THREE   **THE HAWAIIAN OPERATION**   50

CHAPTER FOUR   **SUNDAY MORNING INFAMY**   68

CHAPTER FIVE   **FIRE ON THE WATER**   88

EPILOGUE   **THE AFTERMATH**   108

APPENDICES   **A. MUSTER ROLL OF MARINE DETACHMENT ARIZONA, DECEMBER 1941**   118

B. LIEUTENANT GENERAL T. HOLCOMB, CMC–LETTER TO SIMENSEN FAMILY   120

C. LAMAR CRAWFORD AFFIDAVIT AND CASUALTY ROSTER   121

D. CAPTAIN FRANKLIN VAN VALKENBURGH– LETTER TO DIANE GILLETTE   122

E. PROFILES   123

NOTES   125

BIBLIOGRAPHY   126

INDEX   127

PROLOGUE
And The Band Played On

"This is no drill!"
—Lieutenant Commander Logan Ramsey

THE PETTY OFFICER OF THE WATCH checked the bulkhead clock. It was exactly 0755. He nodded to a signalman, who raised the "prep" flag on the Pearl Harbor Navy Yard water tower.

The water tower stood a hundred and seventy-six feet over the water, giving it a commanding view of the harbor. It had a wooden structure on the top, which was used as a signaling station. The prep signal, a white square in a solid field of blue, is the international flag code for the letter *P*. Although prep can have several meanings, when raised at 0755 it meant that morning colors would be executed in exactly five minutes.

USS *Arizona*'s four-man Marine color guard marched purposely toward the fantail beneath the tautly stretched white canvas awning. The leather soles of their spit-shined shoes struck the teak deck with a measured cadence. Their NCO, a corporal, barked a command and the detail halted crisply at the flagstaff. The field music, a single bugle player, took several precise steps, turned, and raised the bugle to his lips. The others busied themselves unlashing the halyard and attaching its snaps to the flag's grommets. The corporal checked to ensure they were attached properly. He was well aware what would happen if the flag was raised upside down—it would be a career-ending event. He glanced at his watch and noted with satisfaction that they were right on time—0755.

A working party of sailors was securing the awning in preparation for Sunday church service. The petty officer in charge was chiding them to hurry; morning colors would sound in five minutes. All along battleship row, men prepared to raise the Stars and Stripes. Aboard the USS *Nevada*, however, the junior officer of deck (JOOD) was in a sweat trying to determine if the color guard had the correct flag size. He sent a messenger to call over to the *Arizona*, which was moored only twenty to thirty feet away (bow to stern), to find out what size they were using.[1] Unlike *Arizona*'s single bugler, *Nevada*'s entire twenty-three-piece band had mustered in formation on the fantail. The captain of the *Arizona* had given his band permission to sleep in. They had won the first round of "The Battle of Music," a competition among the navy's Pearl Harbor bands.

Marine Major Alan Shapley was up early, even though he didn't have any official duties. He had been relieved as detachment commander the previous day. However, he was the player-coach—and leading hitter—of the ship's baseball team and was scheduled to play that afternoon against the team from the aircraft carrier USS *Enterprise* for the championship of the Pacific Fleet. After dressing, he went to the wardroom for breakfast. He helped himself to a large stack of pancakes, topped with eggs, his favorite weekend breakfast, and joined the ship's doctor, chaplain, and Lieutenant Commander Samuel G. Fuqua, the duty department head, and worked his way through the flapjacks. Below decks, Corporal Earl C. Nightingale was also eating a leisurely breakfast. Around him, the mess deck was alive with lighthearted banter as sailors and Marines of the off-duty section moved through the chow line.

High overhead, Commander Mitsuo Fuchida of the Imperial Japanese Navy led a mixed strike force of fighters, high-level bombers, and torpedo planes toward the unsuspecting Pacific Fleet anchorage. As Fuchida approached Pearl Harbor, he looked down through his binoculars. "What a majestic sight, almost unbelievable. There lay the beautiful harbor with all the great ships at anchor…."[2] At 0749, he ordered his radio operator, 1st Flying Petty Officer Tokunobu Mizuki, to signal: "*To!* [Charge!] *To!* [Charge!] *To!* [Charge!]."

The *Nevada*'s bandmaster raised his baton and swept it down. The first notes of "The Star-Spangled Banner" echoed across the fantail, mixed with the unmistakable scream of a diving aircraft. The Marine color guard quickly raised Old Glory to the top of the flagstaff. Suddenly an unfamiliar plane roared low over *Arizona*, angling sharply upward over the formation. Incredulously, machine-gun bullets spewed from the rear gun, chewing up the teak deck and ripping the flag to shreds—however, "the band played on!" never missing a beat. Miraculously, not a single member was scratched but, on the last obviated note, the formation scattered for cover.

Shapley was just finishing breakfast when, "I heard this terrible bang and crash. I thought it was a motor sailer [a boat powered by engine or sail] that they had dropped on the fantail, and I ran up there to see what it was all about. When I got up on deck . . . I heard a sailor say, 'This is the best damned drill the Army Air Corps has ever put on.' Then I saw a destroyer being blown up in the dry dock across the way." Private First Class Lamar Crawford was on the quarterdeck. "I saw a lone plane head my way. It strafed the color guard! Stray bullets hit the gun mount beside me with 'to whom it may concern' written on them. I ducked back into the Marine compartment." Corporal Nightingale had finished breakfast. "I was just leaving the compartment when the ship's siren sounded 'air defense'. I heard an explosion . . . machine-gun fire . . . and the Marine color guard ran in, saying we were under attack!" he said.

Lieutenant Commander Logan Ramsey, operations officer, Patrol Wing Two on Ford Island, located in the middle of Pearl Harbor, turned to a fellow officer. "That was a Jap plane and a delayed-action bomb."[3] He ordered the radioman to send out a plain English message. "AIR RAID ON PEARL HARBOR. THIS IS NOT DRILL!"

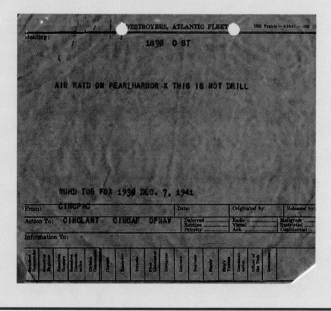

The CincPac message announcing the Japanese raid on Pearl Harbor. *History Division, USMC*

Arizona in 1930 with newly installed fore and aft tripod masts. Note the presidential flag flying from the mainmast.
History Division, USMC

CHAPTER ONE

MARINE DETACHMENT ARIZONA

"[They practiced] gun drills constantly, hours at a time."
—Marine Captain John H. "Jack" Earle

THE MERRY POINT BOAT LANDING, named after Rear Admiral John Merry, buzzed with activity. Marine Captain John H. "Jack" Earle described the landing, located between the navy yard and the submarine base: "When standing in the middle of the landing, a long concrete dock lined with buildings was on the left. On the right, a short planked wood transverse dock led to the submarine base. It was a busy place, [with] liberty parties coming and going and supplies being delivered to the ships." The Pacific Fleet had just returned from maneuvers and had sounded "liberty call." Motor launches crammed with sailors jockeyed for space along the crowded berth. The men were impatient to hit the beach for "Cinderella liberty"—freedom expired at midnight—along Honolulu's notorious Hotel Street. Working parties manhandled jumbled piles of crates and boxes under the watchful eyes of petty officers. Navy officers in crisp whites and Marines in starched khakis strode purposely through the disorder, coming from or going to the dreadnoughts moored in pairs along Pearl Harbor's Ford Island. The open expanse of water between the landing and the great ships echoed with the clamor of the daily routine—high-pitched boatswain's pipes, emergency-signal tests, bugle calls, and the all-pervasive demand, "Now hear this." A slight onshore breeze brought the stench of diesel fuel, overwhelming the flower-scented fragrance of Pearl Harbor's tropical plants.

Twenty-one-year-old Marine Private Henry Kalinowski made his way across the wooden planks of the landing, struggling with the heavy, unwieldy seabag balanced on his shoulder. Sweat stained his khaki uniform. The five-foot nine-inch, blond-haired, blue-eyed poster-boy Marine looked like a "soup sandwich," not the squared-away look of a seagoing Marine. He was reporting to his first duty station, the Marine Detachment, USS *Arizona*, flagship of Battleship Division 1, and he was filled with excitement, wonder, and some anxiety. The seeming confusion on the dock added to his apprehension. He was deeply worried about how he was going to get to the ship; his training at Sea School did not cover this minor detail. Luckily a fifty-foot motor launch, with the letters "ARIZ" on its bow, nudged the landing. A sailor in the bow shouted out, "*Arizona*," a hail for those going to the ship. The coxswain, a boatswain's mate second class, handled the craft with a confident poise. He certainly looked the part to the young Marine—dazzling white uniform, erect posture, and a white "Dixie Cup" hat perched rakishly low on his brow, a regulation two-fingers above the bridge of his nose. With a sigh of relief, Kalinowski and several sailors climbed aboard. He stowed his seabag and settled back for the short ride to the ship.

The boatswain's mate maneuvered beautifully out of the slip, gunned the engine, and headed for the *Arizona*, which was moored to a quay on the east side of Ford Island. As the launch approached the great battleship's port gangway, the coxswain made a neat "two bell" landing ("engine back" and "engine stop"). Two crewmen snared the accommodation ladder with boat hooks and held it steady against the side of the ship. Kalinowski stepped out of the launch onto a small wooden platform, leaving his seabag to be hoisted aboard with the other assorted equipment and baggage. He climbed to the top of the accommodation ladder, came stiffly to attention, faced the flagstaff on the stern, and saluted the National Ensign. He then faced the officer of the deck (OD), who had a telescope under his arm as a distinctive badge of office, and saluted. "Permission to come aboard, sir," he requested. "Permission granted," the young officer responded, returning the salute in the time-honored custom for boarding a man-o'-war.

Similarly, Marine Lieutenant Chester R. Allen remembers coming aboard the USS *Nevada*. "I went to the ship for the first time, which was very confusing. There was a guy blowing a whistle so loud that I couldn't hear, and I had to pass through two sailors that had stepped aside to allow me to proceed up the gangway. Fortunately, I had been taught to salute the colors and then the officer of the deck. This was an entirely new experience, but to end up, it was a very enjoyable one."

The slender Kalinowski stepped onto the whitened teak quarterdeck and announced that he was reporting for duty. The officer nodded and told him to stand fast until an escort arrived. Kalinowski took the opportunity to look around. He was overwhelmed by the sheer size of the gray behemoth, which, twenty-six years after its christening, was five years older than he was. Four huge armored turrets, two forward and two aft, squatted menacingly on the deck. Smaller weapons seemed to project from every nook and cranny. Two enormous steel tripod masts loomed high overhead. He watched a sailor climb slowly up the dizzying height and wondered what it would be like to scurry up the exposed steel rungs in an emergency. Movement caught his eye. He looked aft just in time to see a crane lift a plane into the air and stared spellbound as a Vought OS2U-3 Kingfisher monoplane was gently placed on Turret No. 3. For a young man just three months away from Ashtabula, Ohio, the sights and sounds aboard the man-o'-war were almost indescribable. The ship spoke of power, strength, and a sense of indestructibility. He felt a surge of pride at being part of the USS *Arizona*'s Marine Detachment.

The submarine base looking south. Merry Point landing is in the center, to the right of the smaller storage tanks. Note the submarines moored alongside a sub tender. *National Archives 80-G-451126*

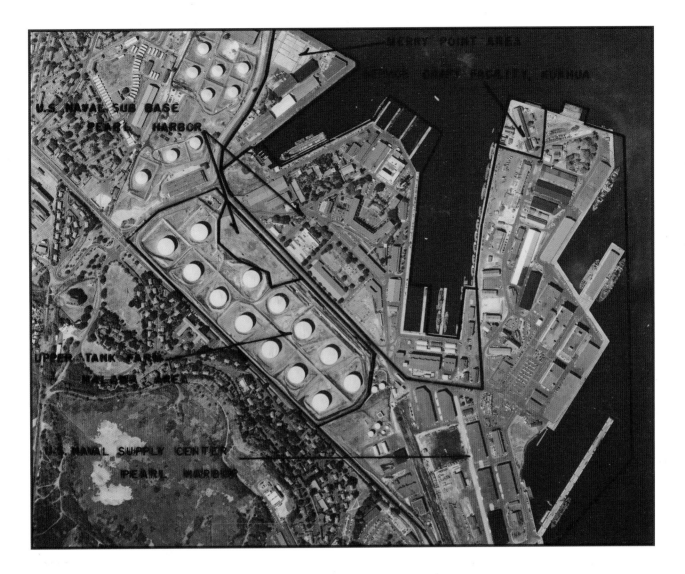

Pearl Harbor's submarine base, located southeast of Ford Island. *History Division, USMC*

Kalinowski's reverie was broken when his escort arrived, a Marine who served as the office runner. The two moved out smartly, passing through several hatches. Kalinowski quickly became disoriented. He also learned a painful lesson that the bottom of a hatch combing is not called a "knee knocker" for nothing. Twice he managed to bark his shins on the unforgiving steel. They finally arrived at the detachment's administrative office, an eight-by-ten-foot compartment, where the senior enlisted man of the detachment held sway.

First Sergeant John Duveene was an old Corps regular whose service spanned over two and a half decades. He had served "wherever a Marine could tote a gun," from the trenches of France to unpronounceable backwater foreign ports. The "Top" was firm but fair—a man the youngsters of the detachment could look to for guidance, direction, and, above all, motivation. He called the Marines of the detachment his "champions." As a first sergeant, he was responsible for the efficient administration of the detachment's paperwork, but, woe to the man who called him a paper pusher. First Sergeant Duveene thought of himself, first and foremost, as a leader, a "field Marine," even though administration was his forte. In fact, during a surprise admiral's inspection in June, his area received special mention: "Administration Marine Detachment considered excellent; all records accurately kept and up to date."

Formal *Arizona* Marine detachment photo, taken in 1920. Marine officers and senior noncommissioned officers are seated front and center with swords. *History Division, USMC*

Duveene quickly and expertly entered Kalinowski on the muster roll—the Holy Grail of personnel reports. After completing the forms, he briefed the youngster on the detachment. Eighty-seven Marines were attached to *Arizona*, five officers, eighteen non-commissioned officers, and sixty-four nonrated men (as of the December muster roll). The detachment was organized into "two platoons and a small company headquarters for drills, combat exercises, parades, and landing force. For routine duty aboard ship the organization conforms to the usual ship's bill of two watches." The detachment served as orderlies for the ship's senior naval officers—admiral, captain, executive officer, as well as brig sentry, lifebuoy sentry, gangway sentries, and fire guards. But most importantly, they served as gunners for the 5-inch 51-caliber secondary batteries.

An unknown Marine detachment first sergeant. As senior enlisted man, the first sergeant functioned as father-confessor, disciplinarian, and leader. *Author's collection*

During the conversation, Duveene learned that the Ohio native had joined, like so many others of his generation, to escape the Depression's grinding poverty and lack of opportunity. Kalinowski's family was forced to split up and move in with relatives. His cousin Ken said, "I thought he was my brother; he lived with us for a while. I just considered him my big brother." He described Henry as "a happy-go-lucky youth. He was always telling jokes and teasing me." After graduating from high school, Kalinowski worked for the Works Progress Administration, a massive employment relief program that paid a salary of only ten dollars a week. It offered little in the way of a future. In March 1941, Kalinowski left his extended family to join the Corps. His sister Josephine remembered, "He went in because he wanted to better himself. He thought the Marines was the best—he'd get a good education there and he'd come out as a professional." On the day he left, he bought her a big bag of candy. He kissed her on the cheek and said, "I'll see you later, kiddo." It was the last time she would see him.

Duveene completed the paperwork and led the newest member of the detachment to meet its commander, thirty-eight-year-old Captain Alan Shapley, a 1927 graduate of the Naval Academy. Shapley had been the commander for a year and was due for transfer in the winter of 1941. He recently learned that he had been selected for promotion, and he expected to pin on the gold oak leaves of a major in a few weeks. He had served in a variety of posts and stations—Marine Barracks, Pearl Harbor, aide-de-camp, commanding officer Marine Detachment USS *San Francisco*—and had excelled in each. The *Arizona* tour marked him as an officer with a bright future. It was well known that a tour at sea was a leg up for promotion, particularly service on a ship with an admiral on board. Captain Earle claimed, "The best of the best went to sea and the best of them went to the flagship." It did not hurt that Shapley was a Naval Academy graduate, could "speak navy" with his "ring knocker" contemporaries, and that his father was a serving naval officer.

Shapley was an outgoing officer with a down-to-earth style of leadership. He spoke plainly, straight from the shoulder. His men knew what he expected and tried to give it to him. It did not pay to cross swords with the "old man." Even so, he was well liked. Private Russell McCurdy described Shapley as "a superb leader that took a genuine interest in the men of the detachment. He knew our records and our personalities and treated us

Long before being assigned to the *Arizona* at Pearl Harbor, a young Lieutenant Alan Shapley served at the Pearl Harbor Marine Barracks from January 1929 to October 1931. *History Division, USMC*

with respect. Unlike the stereotypical Marine in command, Shapley was not the gruff type. He was soft-spoken and economical in his use of words, but he got the message across."

Shapley also had an excellent professional rapport with the two senior NCOs. The three shared a mutual respect and love of the Corps. Tall and physically fit, a member of the detachment described Shapley as a "well-built boxer of tremendous strength." Shapley loved sports. He was a standout athlete at the Naval Academy and brought that competitive spirit to the *Arizona*. He encouraged his men to participate on the ship's athletic teams as a way to combat boredom, as well as to stay in shape. In addition, intramural sports were big business in the fleet, where ships competed fiercely for trophies and bragging rights. One Marine officer said that his

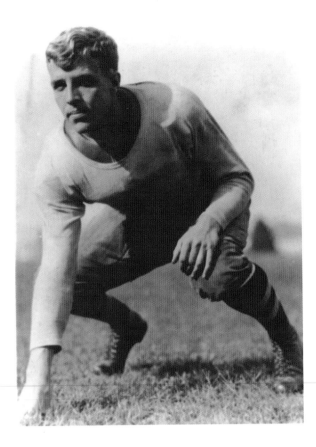

Midshipman Alan Shapley in football stance. *History Division, USMC*

of that team, and I enjoyed that because we won the battleship championship. That was fun too!" He also refereed the fleet's boxing smokers.

During the annual rifle and pistol training, 92 percent of Shapley's Marines qualified in one of three categories—expert, sharpshooter, or marksman—a respectful percentage. In addition, seven members were on *Arizona*'s rifle and pistol team. (Three members were aboard *Arizona* on December 7; Sergeant John M. Baker survived, but Sergeant Charles W. Cole and Private Eugene Brickley did not.) Shapley also instructed the ship's landing force—sailors assigned to augment the Marine detachment for operations ashore—in firing small arms and infantry tactics. However, the instruction was often an exercise in futility. One detachment commander allowed that it was a hopeless proposition—a complete waste of time because the sailors "didn't want to play."

One of Shapley's primary duties included controlling the Marine 5-inch 51-caliber secondary batteries. The position was located in the fire control station, known as secondary aft, atop the mainmast where Kalinowski had watched the sailor climb the tripod. The station consisted of a three-level cupola that contained the main and secondary battery directors, one above the other, some

commanding officer didn't like Marines until they won the Battenberg Cup—named after its donor, British First Sea Lord Prince Louis of Battenberg—a symbol of athletic supremacy. Afterward the commander became their strongest supporter.

Shapley's 1941 detachment annual report noted that his Marines played on the swimming, baseball, boxing, basketball, golf, and bowling teams (golf team member Private Gilbert H. Whisler was killed on December 7). He was proud that the softball team won the interdivision competition and the basketball team won first place. The Marine whaleboat crew won bragging rights by finishing as runner-up in the Battleship Division 1 raceboat competition, a navy specialty (eleven of the thirteen members in the crew were killed in action). Shapley persuaded the ship's captain to allow the Marine team to continue to represent the ship.

He was always involved in sports. "It was fun; I had the [ship's] baseball team. I was the coach and first baseman

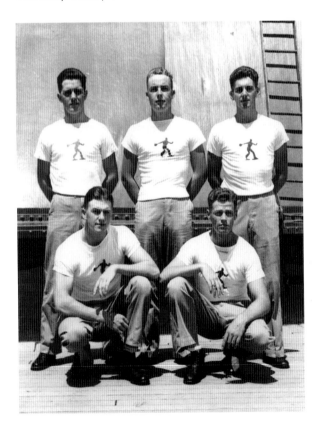

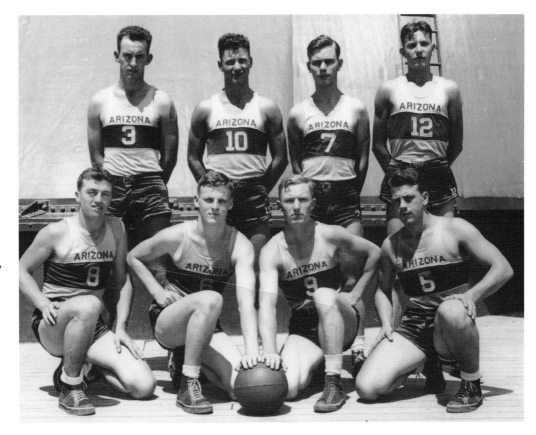

Among other sports, Shapley's 1941 Marine detachment was active in the *Arizona*'s intramural bowling (opposite page), basketball, and whaleboat teams. *History Division, USMC*

one hundred feet above the main deck. Shapley's station was located on the lower level. During firing practice or general quarters, Shapley, the detachment executive officer, First Lieutenant John P. Coursey, and twenty enlisted Marines manned the station. They had to climb the outside tripod leg—ship's traffic pattern required starboard up, port down—and enter through a hatch in the bottom of the cupola. At night or in heavy weather, manning the station was not for the faint of heart. Lieutenant Wilburt S. "Bigfoot" Brown related an incident that occurred on the USS *Pennsylvania*. "I had a recruit ahead of me on the ladder who was scared of heights and froze. People were behind me and this man wouldn't move. He closed his eyes and clung on for dear life. There was only one thing I could do, so I knocked him out. As he collapsed, I caught him, threw him over my shoulder, and carried him to the top. Needless to say, that was the last time he climbed the mast—I found a place for him on the deck."

John Coursey, a native of Georgia, was a former army second lieutenant who transferred to the Corps because, he said, "I thought I would like the Marines." He was no stranger to the *Arizona*, having served aboard her from May 1938 to 1939. A third officer, Second Lieutenant Carleton Elliott "Sim" Simensen, was almost as "fresh caught" as Kalinowski. He attended the University of North Dakota, where he was the top ROTC graduate. After commissioning, he attended the Basic School at Philadelphia, graduating in February 1941. He went home for a short leave and then was assigned to recruiting duty in the upper Midwest for three months. In late

May he sailed aboard the USS *Curtis* for Pearl Harbor and joined *Arizona* in mid-June. In the short time he was aboard, Simensen had already established a good rapport with the detachment. Private First Class James E. Cory described him as "one of the most popular officers on the *Arizona*." A fellow officer described him as "a fairly quiet, self-effacing man who had great people skills and strong leadership qualities."

During the meeting with Kalinowski, Shapley found the youngster to be well-spoken and intelligent, just the type of Marine who would do well on sea duty. He also discovered that he was an excellent bowler—the city of Ashtabula counted him among their best—and encouraged him to join the team. After cautioning him about the usual three distractions that a young man could encounter—booze, broads, and boredom—Shapley turned him over to the first sergeant for assignment to one of the gun crews that was shorthanded. Kalinowski's size and strength was just what was needed to manhandle the fifty-pound shell. With that, Private Henry Kalinowski officially joined the Marine Detachment, USS *Arizona*.

Duveene took Kalinowski back to the office on the boat deck, next to the Marine compartment, where the detachment "gunny" waited. Master Gunnery Sergeant Walter Holzworth was a Corps legend. The men of the detachment adored him. Captain Earle said that Holzworth "saved my ass many times—but that's what a good non-commissioned officer should do for a young second lieutenant." He described Holzworth as "not big or brawny, rather he was quiet and subdued, but with great

Marines of the *Arizona's* landing force, circa 1919. Note the blanket roll across shoulder, cartridge belt, canteen, and leggings. Early Marines wore the campaign cover (the Smokey Bear–style hat) with the Marine emblem (eagle, globe, and anchor) on the crown. *Author's collection* Below: The *Arizona* in heavy seas; the tripod masts date this photo to after her 1930 refit. *History Division, USMC*

command presence." Earle related a story about his friend when they were stationed together in a machine-gun platoon at Quantico. "The men were across the street from the barracks, practicing with blank ammunition. Upon completion of the exercise, Holzworth brought the platoon back to the basement of the barracks to clean weapons. Suddenly a shot rang out. The company commander and I ran to the basement, to find the dimly lit room filled with cordite smoke. The CO confronted Holzworth and angrily demanded, 'Who fired that shot?' Holzworth looked him in the eye and with great aplomb said, 'What shot, sir?' The officer stared at him for the longest time and then said, 'Oh, Goddamit Holzworth,' turned, and left the room."

Lieutenant General Victor Krulak served with Holzworth and described him as "a classic Marine, who had seen every side of the Corps, from the 1st Aviation Company in World War I to the Fleet Marine Force. With service 'in far-off foreign lands'—China, Haiti, Guam—and in the continental posts of the Corps—Norfolk, Quantico, San Diego, Lakehurst, Philadelphia—he epitomized the hard professional Marine, the beau ideal of every new wearer of the Globe and Anchor, myself included." According to General Krulak, the gunny offered a bit of homespun philosophy on how to get along with *Arizona*'s Marine commander: " 'Gunny, I want to make a success of this profession. Tell me how to get along with the captain,' [I said.] 'It's easy, Lieutenant,' the old veteran said, 'Just find out what the old SOB wants, and give it to him.' " Krulak remembered, "I never forgot that advice. And you'll find Holzworth's name on that white tablet out there at Pearl Harbor."

Kalinowski soon found himself lugging his gear to the Marine compartment. It ran the width of the ship and was the detachment's sleeping quarters, mess hall, office, and a place to relax when not on duty. In quick succession he was issued several items of organizational property, including a navy-issue hammock and a space to sling it. The junior enlisted men slept in canvas hammocks slung from hooks fixed to vertical stanchions that extended from deck to overhead. The hammocks were suspended about six feet off the deck, which required the man to grab an I-beam in the overhead and swing up into it, rather than climb in. Admittedly, sleeping in a hammock took some getting used to, as many could attest to after tumbling out onto the steel deck.

Senior Marines used folding cots that were set up each night. The cots and hammocks were stored in bins alongside the forward and starboard bulkheads of the compartment during the day. Captain Earle recalled walking through the dimly lit area at night: "The Marine crews slept in the compartment by rigging hammocks from hooks in the overhead. The sleeping men were a sight to see under the dim blue battle lights; they looked like mummies." Personal effects—primarily uniforms and toilet articles—were stored in small passageway lockers, fourteen inches wide, twenty inches high, and fourteen inches deep. There was no need for larger spaces because the men did not have much in the way of personal effects and did not need a large storage area.

One of Kalinowski's first assignments involved mess cooking, a chore all junior enlisted men performed. At mealtime, mess cooks slid tables and benches down steel poles from storage in the overhead. Stainless-steel eating utensils, heavy porcelain plates, and handleless cups were laid out. The mess cook retrieved the food from the main galley and brought it back to the compartment, where it was served family style. Most meals had some sort of dessert—pie, cookies, or pudding. The senior man at the table was responsible for conduct. In some messes, a man had to ask permission to take the food as it was passed. After the meal, the mess cook raised the table and benches and cleaned the dishes. The detachment had only sixty-two junior enlisted men—thirty-seven PFCs and twenty privates, which meant that mess duty came around all too frequently. As an incentive, mess cooks got an extra five dollars per month, which for a private meant a 25 percent increase in pay. Kalinowski got off a stint of mess duty on December 6, 1941.

Firing the Batteries

For battleships—ships of the line—guns represented the reason for their existence. In the early twentieth century, naval strategists envisioned a grand battle between capital ships, as exemplified by the Battle of Jutland in 1916. The German High Seas Fleet and the British Grand Fleet fought the largest surface action of the era, which led the navies of the world to continue building bigger and heavier armed warships.

John Seymour Letcher, as a young officer, served aboard the battleship USS *Oklahoma*. He theorized that "the sole reason for the existence of a battleship is to carry its guns so that they can be brought to bear upon an enemy. If the guns aren't fired rapidly and accurately, the ship is of little value. So, gunnery was the thing of the greatest importance on a battleship."

Navy Hammocks

Berthing space was always at a premium. Early man-o'-wars solved the problem by using hammocks (introduced to Europeans by Christopher Columbus after he saw West Indian natives use the swinging beds). The hammocks were suspended from hooks that were welded to the overhead deck supports. End rings were slipped over the hooks and cinched tight with a knotted line. A notched wooden stick, 1x1x16 inches, was placed between the two outside lines to keep the hammock from folding around the sleeper. In rough weather old salts swore that a hammock "rode better" than a cot, which mimicked the movement of the ship.

Arizona's main battery consisted of 14-inch 45-caliber naval guns mounted in four three-gun turrets. In this usage, *caliber* refers to the length of the gun expressed in units of its bore, the internal diameter of the barrel. Thus the barrel of a 14-inch 45-caliber gun is 45 times 14 inches in length, or 630 inches (52.5 feet) overall. Each gun was some 46 inches in outside diameter at the breech and weighed more than seventy tons. The gun tubes were rifled to improve accuracy; spiral grooves in the barrel imparted a spin to the projectile giving it a right hand twist of one revolution for each 37.3 feet of travel.

The gunhouse, the visible part of the turret, rotated on roller bearings within a fixed armored tube or barbette that extended through several decks, deep into the ship. Each of the massive guns weighed sixty-two tons and was more than fifty feet in length. Each round that was fired eroded the liner of the barrel, which had to be replaced after 175 rounds.

It took four hundred pounds of gunpowder (four silk bags) to fire a 1,500 pound armor-piercing shell twenty-three thousand yards (approximately thirteen miles). Each turret required seventy men to service it—twenty-five in the turret and forty-five to man the ammunition hoists and the magazines, the ammunition storage compartments. It was not easy to become a member of a gun crew. Seaman 2nd Class John Rampley recalled the procedure. "A man's name was presented by the senior petty officer to the whole gun crew. If any of them didn't like him or thought he wouldn't be compatible, you didn't get in. So, if you did make it, you felt that you were part of a select crew."

Firing Ballet

There was a subdued excitement in the turret as the gun crew waited for the signal to fire. Months of effort had gone into this moment. They had morphed from a ragged bunch of individuals into a close-knit, well-trained gun crew that wanted the opportunity to prove it. Suddenly the warning bell sounded, and the men braced themselves in positions away from the recoil of the gun—the sudden backward movement of sixty-two tons would crush a careless man. High above them, in the foremast, the gunnery officer pressed a button, closing a circuit. The main battery fired.

Inside the turret, the gun crew quickly reloaded in a choreographed ballet of precision movement. Gun pointers leveled the gun to line up with the loading trays. The breeches were opened by the gun captains, and compressed air was blown into the chamber to clear any smoldering propellant remnants. Without proper maintenance, fumes from the previous firing could ignite and explode back into the gunhouse; similarly, embers from the previous firing could ignite the powder bags for the next round.

The first loader, using a mechanical hoist, transferred a shell onto the loading tray, while the second loader extended the loading tray into the breech. An electric rammer pushed the projectile forward until its brass rotating band engaged the lands of the barrel's rifling. Powder bags, weighing 105 pounds each, were muscled onto the loading tray and then pushed into the gun chamber with a ten-foot wooden pole. The pole had a leather pad on one end to prevent sparks. Finally, the gun captain closed the breech and inserted a .44-caliber primer cartridge into the firing lock. The turret officer pushed a button to convey a ready status. It was expected that a good gun crew would average forty-five seconds between rounds, depending on training, equipment status, and sea state.

In the ammunition storage compartment, the magazine crew pushed the 1,500- pound shell along overhead rails by a chain inserted into a padeye, a metal ring in the

Blowback

In 1924, the USS *Mississippi* suffered a catastrophic fire during a battle practice that killed forty-seven crewmen. Seven salvos had been fired from the right gun of Turret No. 2. Just after the eighth salvo had been rammed, a small gray mass of smoke and flame came out of the breech, followed immediately by a blinding flash. Fire and gas filled the gun compartments and passed through the safety doors into the other gun compartments, the upper handling room, and the turret officer's booth. An investigation concluded that the bore had not been inspected properly after firing (burning embers were still present) and that the safety doors had not been properly closed.

On July 24, 1936, the *Arizona* was firing its main battery when Turret No. 2 had a blowback. It occurred when the breech of the right gun was pulled open. Bore gases came back into the gun chamber, expanded, and burst into flame. The turret officer saw the sheet of flame and dense smoke and activated the sprinkling system. His quick action saved the turret from a possible catastrophic explosion. One seaman was burned but not seriously.

base of the projectile. The round was then hoisted up a tube into the turret. The propellant charges, silk bags filled with black powder, were stored in metal containers, two to a can, in the powder magazine. The bags were taken from the metal containers and passed through a scuttle (to limit the danger of fire), placed on a hoist, and lifted into the turret. A red felt pad covered one end of each powder bag; behind the pad was the ignition charge of black powder. In case of a broken powder bag, everyone in the turret was to freeze and carefully submerge the loose grains in containers of water that had been strategically placed in the turret. Slightly torn bags were restitched on the spot. To fire the gun, a primerman inserted a primer about the size of a shotgun shell into the breech. Usually an electrical circuit fired the primer into the ignition pad. This ignition set off the smokeless powder that produced the explosion that fired the projectile.

Secondary Battery

The location of the Marine compartment was close to the gun casemates, their battle stations. Half the *Arizona*'s secondary batteries were manned by Marines. In the June 1941 annual report, Shapley recorded that "during the period 1 July, to 31 December, 1940, the Marine Detachment manned six (6) 5-inch 51-caliber guns." The secondary batteries were designed for defense against destroyer-launched torpedo attacks and were distributed in casemates on the main deck. A casemate was a twelve-by-twenty-foot compartment that housed a 5-inch 51-caliber gun and its crew. It had an embrasure to accommodate training of the gun in an arc of fire between 90 degrees and 120 degrees. The convex gun port's outer bulkhead enabled it to traverse in a wide angle of fire. However, the vertical opening limited the gun's elevation to 20 degrees, preventing it from being used in an antiaircraft mode. *Arizona*'s casemates had a canvas curtain to close off the casemate in normal weather. In heavy seas, it had metal shutters to seal them off. Rubber gaskets prevented water from leaking past the shutter's seams.

Each casement had either a Marine noncommissioned officer or a navy petty officer gun captain. *Arizona*'s gun captains, four sergeants and two corporals, were all rated second class. They received $2.50 extra per month (a princely sum considering that base pay for a private was only $21.00) and were authorized to wear a distinctive insignia—the symbol of a cannon on the sleeve of their blue-and-green blouse. Corporal Burnis Leroy Bond was a typical gun captain. He was a squared-away slow-talking Mississippian, with a drawl so pronounced that boys from north of the Mason-Dixon had trouble understanding him. However, Bond spoke Holzworth's language well enough for the gunny to recommend him for a ship warrant (upon transfer he would revert to PFC) to corporal. Bond had shown he had the right stuff, working his way up through the gun crew—loader, pointer, director, and finally gun captain He ran a tight ship, working his gun crew hard and using every spare moment to practice. PFC James E. Cory was the pointer on Bond's gun crew. He recalled that for weeks on end "the *Arizona* was at sea for target practice and ship maneuvers."

Captain Jack Earle remembered *Arizona*'s Marines "practicing gun drills constantly, hours at a time—using a loading machine." The machine consisted of a steel framework that supported a working model of a breech-block. An officer remarked that "the enlisted men were drilled for interminable hours into teams of near inhuman perfection." A well-trained gun crew could fire eight to nine rounds per minute.

Earle related an incident that occurred during a night shoot. The main battery fired, sending heavy vibrations through the casemates. A large metal container of pepper, stored on a narrow ledge in the overhead, dislodged and crashed to the deck, spilling its contents into the air. The gun crew immediately started tearing up and sneezing uncontrollably, which they were forced to endure because they couldn't leave their general quarters station.

Bond's number-ten gun was located on the starboard side of the ship, adjacent to gun number eight. Guns five, seven, and nine were on the port side. His crew consisted of eleven men, most of whom were ammunition and powder handlers. The guns were serviced by hoists, which brought ammunition and powder to the casemates from below decks. Each shell weighed fifty pounds and was painted to assist the gun crews in identifying the type of shell, yellow for explosive and black for armor piercing. Twenty-five pounds of black powder propelled the shell out to a range of eight miles.

The loading crew stood in two lines, shell men on the left and powder men on the right, forming a V, with the breech at the point of the V. The men were timed with stopwatches, and those who didn't measure up were transferred to less demanding positions.

Captain John S. Letcher, USS *Oklahoma*, described how the 5-inch 51-caliber broadside battery was aimed: "The guns were kept pointed at the target by the pointer on the right side of the gun, who moved it vertically up and down to compensate for the rolling of the ship, and by the trainer on the left side who moved it horizontally. These men guided the movement of the gun by looking through telescopic sights mounted on the gun carriage. There were crosshairs in the telescopes, and if the gun was properly bore-sighted it was pointed at the target when the intersection of the crosshairs was centered on the target."

The Marine secondary batteries were controlled from the battery director's station located in the mainmast, known as "secondary aft." It towered a hundred feet over the water and could be reached only by climbing a steel ladder on the outside of the tripod. The battery control station had both a port and starboard director and was staffed by as many as forty men. Both Shapley and Coursey were school-trained directors. They had attended the Fleet Secondary Battery Gunnery School

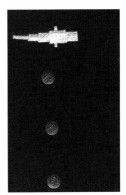

Gun captain's cannon insignia on the sleeve of a Marine formal "dress blues" uniform, just above the buttoned cuff. *Author's collection*

Marine gunners of the USS *New York. History Division, USMC*

and the .50-caliber Anti-Aircraft Gunnery School aboard the *Nevada*, where they learned the intricacies of fire control. Earle described the control procedures: "The target's position was electronically transmitted to the gun crews by using two identical dials—one in the director's station and the other in the casemate—called a 'repeater.' The gun crew dial had a designator called a 'bug,' which noted the position of the target. They were always chided to 'follow the bug' when firing." Earle noted that he was drilled to "fire on the uproll," a term that survived from the earliest days of naval warfare— fire as the ship rolls upward in the wave action.

Commence Firing

"The precision and speed and teamwork of a well-trained broadside gun crew made it a thing of beauty to watch," John Letcher nostalgically remembered. "At the command 'Commence Firing,' the gun captain, standing to the right rear of the breech, swung the breechblock out of the breech and with his left hand inserted a primer into the primer vent of the block. The instant that the breechblock had swung out of the breech the tray man, who had been crouching just behind the gun on the left side, inserted the tray, which resembled an iron bucket with the bottom removed, into the breech. As he did so the first shell man, a husky fellow who had been standing just behind the tray man, sprang forward. He held the nose of the fifty-pound projectile nestled in the crook of the elbow of his left arm, and with his right hand resting on the base he thrust the projectile forward into the breech with the motion and force of a man putting the shot. An instant later the rammer man, using a wooden rammer of about the thickness of a baseball bat and twice as long, rammed the projectile home to seat it in the chamber. As his rammer was withdrawn, the first powder man, who was just behind the gun captain on the right side of the V, thrust the bag of powder—which was two and a half feet long and four and a half inches in diameter—into the breech behind the projectile. As he did this, the tray was withdrawn and the gun captain slammed the breechblock shut to close the chamber. An instant later when the electric buzzer was sounding, the pointer pressed the trigger, which was a part of his elevating gear wheel, and the gun fired."

First Lieutenant Chester Allen related a story about a well-trained crew: "As the firing proceeded, the first shell man dropped the shell and the powder man, just in unison, pushed the powder bag into the breach. The

gun fired the blank charge. As soon as the firing was over, the gun captain went over, picked up the shell, and tossed it out the gun port, as if nothing had happened. He then reported to the officer, 'All ammunition expended, no casualties.'"

Shapley encouraged a healthy rivalry among the gun crews, particularly between his Marines and the sailors. The rivalry culminated each September, when the ship's gunnery prowess was officially tested during the short-range battle practice. It was conducted in designated firing areas, outside the normal shipping lanes. The target was made of gray canvas, twelve feet square, mounted on a raft, and towed by a ship moving in the opposite direction. The rules governing the shoot were strict and carefully observed by neutral umpires. It was the goal of each gun crew to win the navy "E" for excellence. If a maximum score was achieved, the crew could paint a large white "E" on their casemate and wear a cloth "E" on the sleeve of their uniforms. They might also be in line for prize money and promotion. Lieutenant Allen recalled that *Nevada* had an excellent gunnery department. "We got the gunnery 'E,' which was painted on the ship's smokestack. This was quite an honor because the Pacific Fleet at that time was pretty big. The following year *Nevada* was designated the broadside gunnery school for the entire fleet." Allen mentioned that on one particularly bad day, the ship's gunnery officer swore over an open circuit. "Je-sus Christ," he exclaimed. A few seconds later an anonymous voice responded, "Jesus Christ, aye, aye."

Shapley noted in his annual report, "At short range battle practice held August 28, 1940, there were no 'E' guns. The results attained by the Marine .50-cal machine gun crews were well above the average attained by the ship, although no 'Es' were awarded." So, while his detachment didn't win the coveted "E," they did win bragging rights over their navy counterparts. Second Lieutenant Victor "Brute" Krulak described the short-range battle practice as "essentially familiarization training for the crew and was like shooting fish in a barrel." During his time on the *Arizona*, he remembered that "the ship's secondary battery was accurate enough to score frequent hits at ranges of eight to ten thousand yards." Letcher did not enjoy that level of success. "We always had high hopes of every gun making an 'E' but they never did. The practice always followed the same pattern, high hopes and disappointing results . . . they should have been called 'The Annual Disappointment'!"

The Marine officer in the foreground holds a stopwatch to time the crew during gun practice. *History Division, USMC*

Marines of the USS *New York* move supplies below decks near a turret. A corporal, standing just behind the crate, supervises. *History Division, USMC*

The USS *Pennsylvania*, the *Arizona*'s sister ship, entering Pearl Harbor through the channel. *History Division, USMC*

CHAPTER TWO

FROM REVOLUTION TO PEARL HARBOR

"If it comes to a fight, I want to be in at the start. That's where the Marines belong."

—Master Gunnery Sergeant Walter Holzworth
USS *Arizona*, Pearl Harbor

Marines consider November 10, 1775, their birthday, although the Corps was not officially established until July 11, 1798, when the Continental Congress authorized the raising of two battalions of Marines, who were to be "good seamen or so acquainted with maritime affairs as to be able to serve to advantage at sea . . . and they be distinguished by the names of the First and Second Battalion of Marines."

Samuel Nicholas, a wealthy Quaker innkeeper, was commissioned a captain of Marines on November 28, 1775. Seven months later, Congress placed Nicholas "at the head of the Marines with the rank of Major." He is considered the first commandant. Tun Tavern, a local watering hole in Philadelphia, was selected as the recruiting venue for the new unit. Prospective recruits were lured with offers of prize money, rations, and ample grog as an incentive to enlist. The effort was so successful that the tavern's proprietor was commissioned a captain and became one of the principal recruiting officers during the Revolution.

The new "sea soldiers" were immediately assigned to ships of the Continental Navy, where they participated in several naval battles, including the famous engagement between John Paul Jones' *Bonhomme Richard* and the HMS *Serapis* off the coast of England in 1779. Marines brought credit upon the Corps by climbing into the rigging and delivering a murderous fire upon the British gun crews, driving them from the open deck. Jones mentioned their service in his diary: "At all times they sustain and protect the stern [officer quarters] and necessary

A Marine detachment awaiting orders, circa 1890s. Note the precision of the stacked rifles. *History Division, USMC*

discipline of a ship by their organization, distinctive character, training and, we might add, nature. [They] seconded us bravely; by means of musquetry and swivels; and also threw a multitude of grenades."

The battle was touch and go. At its height, a gutsy Scottish-American sailor crawled out on *Richard*'s main yard with a lighted match and a basket of grenades ". . . until exactly above the enemy's deck." He lighted the fuse, judged the roll of the wallowing ships, and scored a bull's-eye by dropping the grenade down a scuttle. "[It] set fire to the cartridge of an eighteen-pounder . . . [and] the discharge scorched several of the crew," whereupon the British commander surrendered his ship. Casualties were severe on both ships; more than one-third of the crews were killed and wounded, including sixty-seven Marines on the *Richard*.

In the Revolutionary War navy, primitive medical treatment was often worse than the wound itself. The weapons of the day—cannons, muskets, and swords, to say nothing of wooden splinters—caused horrendous wounds, for which amputation was the standard treatment. Each ship had its surgeon, of varying professional qualifications, and loblolly boys, the forerunners of today's navy corpsman. The term "loblolly" was originally the name for a thick gruel that was served to patients in sickbay and also the nautical term for medi-cine. It is thought that the boys who served the food were called loblolly boys. Their job was to spread sand on the deck to soak up blood, retrieve the wounded, fill buckets of water to hold severed limbs, and heat tar to cauterize stumps. They were often pressed into service to hold the wounded man down; painkiller—rum or opium—was not always available. The sights, sounds, and smells that greeted the casualties were unnerving: the surgeon's lair often resembled a blood-spattered abattoir, lanterns threw grotesque shadows in the dimly lit sickbay, and the moans and screams of the wounded, and above all the unforgettable rasping of the bone saw, filled the air.

The duties assigned to the seagoing Continental Marines remained basically the same for the next 150 years. Marine author Colonel John W. Thomason described their duties. "Aboard ship, besides forming the nucleus of the ship's landing force, they man the secondary batteries, the five-inch guns; furnish guards of honor for the comings and goings of the admiral and distinguished visitors, and so forth; perform all manner of curious and annoying details; and post ship's sentries whose meticulous ideas about the enforcement of orders lacerate the souls of jolly mariners, seamen, and engineer ratings."

In the early days of the Republic, Marines were billeted between the crew and the officers and served as the ship's policemen, which on occasion put them at odds with their bluejacket shipmates. They were used to enforce discipline and discourage mutinies, which were not at all uncommon in the eighteenth-century navy. When a ship was captured, Marines were part of the prize crew. The most famous example involved twenty-three-year-old Marine Lieutenant John Marshall Gamble of the *Essex* in 1813. Gamble, with a prize crew of fourteen Marines and seamen, took command of a captured enemy ship. In an incredible display of leadership and courage, Gamble captured a British raider in a sea battle, put down a native uprising, and survived being cast adrift and wounded by mutinous prisoners, before making his way back home.

Marines also served as orderlies to the ship's senior officers, a tradition that continued into the twentieth century, as when Private Dutch Holland served as one of Admiral Nimitz's orderlies. His duties included being a messenger, runner, and bodyguard—and some-time babysitter. Holland and other orderlies were sometimes detailed to play games with Nimitz's seven-year-old daughter, Mary. On one occasion the orderly could not cooperate.

Mary saw him standing duty outside the admiral's cabin and said, "Come in and play with me."

"I can't," he told her. "I'm on duty."

"You'd better," she replied. "My daddy owns this ship, and he'll fire you."

To the Shores of Tripoli

In the early nineteenth century, detachments were assigned to the ship's gunnery division, which began a long history of manning the secondary batteries. Marines were hired on for the princely sum of six dollars per month and an allowance of twenty-eight cents per day for food. They were also provided a uniform and equipment—after a fashion, because much of it was army surplus or hand-me-downs, a practice that continued well into the twentieth century. A leather stock or neckpiece was one uniform item unique to Marines, earning them the nickname "leatherneck." Men were required to wear

A Marine sergeant giving his men "the word"—passing information. *History Division, USMC*

their hair in a queue, or pigtail, powdered with flour—one pound per man per month. A parsimonious supply officer prescribed that it be *sour* flour!

Marines were also used as landing parties to protect American interests ashore because, under international law, they could be landed to protect the lives and property of nationals without a declaration of war. On May 10, 1801, the Pasha of Tripoli declared war on the United States and, a few days later in the ultimate insult, cut down the flagstaff of the American consulate. An American expedition was mounted to assuage the affront. Marine Lieutenant Presley Neville O'Bannon, one sergeant, and six privates accompanied a motley force of sixty-seven Greek mercenaries and one hundred Arabs across six hundred miles of trackless desert. After a grueling seven-week march, enlivened by starvation, mutiny, and sickness, the expedition arrived at the walls of the Pasha's fort at Derna, Tripoli. After the garrison refused to surrender, "Mr. O'Bannon . . . surged forward with his Marines, Greeks, and Arabs . . . passed through a shower of musketry from the walls of houses, took possession of the [enemy] battery, planted the American Flag upon its ramparts, and turned its guns upon the enemy. . . ." It marked the first time an American officer raised the Stars and Stripes over a captured fortress in the old world.[1] Two of O'Bannon's Marines were killed during the assault. The famous exploit is commemorated in the second line of the Marines' hymn—"To the Shores of Tripoli." For his bravery, O'Bannon was presented a Mameluke sword, which with little variation, has been carried by Marine officers ever since.

Remember the *Maine*

At 2110 on the evening of February 1898, Marine Fifer H. C. Newton took position on the quarterdeck and raised his bugle. Navy Captain Charles D. Sigsbee wrote: "I laid down my pen to listen to the notes of the bugle, which were singularly beautiful in the oppressive stillness of the night. The Marine bugler, Newton, who was rather given to fanciful efforts, was evidently doing his best. During his pauses the echoes floated back to the ship with singular distinctness, repeating the strains of the bugle fully and exactly." Lieutenant Albertus W. Catlin, the Marine commander, was trying to find something to write with, so he could pen a letter to a friend. Corporal Frank G. Thompson was settling down in his hammock, which he had rigged on deck. Suddenly, a terrific explosion erupted, killing most of the *Maine*'s crew, including Fifer Newton, and left the ship sinking by the head.

Thompson was thrown out of his hammock. "I don't remember anything but a roar, the shock wave, and a split second of motionless[ness] as I looked down on the superstructure." Private William Anthony, the captain's orderly, made his way below deck, through passageways filled with smoke and flame, to locate his officer. Finding him, Anthony came to attention, saluted, and reported calmly, "Sir, I have to inform you that the ship has been blown up and is sinking." Anthony's devotion to duty in the face of great danger made him an instant hero—and a meritorious sergeant.

America claimed that Spain had blown up the ship and reacted with fury. Congress declared war, using the slogan "Remember the *Maine*" to whip up popular support. The battleship *Maine* became a symbol of enemy treachery, as would *Arizona* four decades later. The U.S. victory over Spain forced Spain out of the Americas and put the United States in power in the Philippines.

The Marines Come of Age

The Spanish-American War signaled the country's emergence as a world power. As wooden ships gave way to steel and steam, the U.S. Navy became an instrument to project power, which transformed the mission of the Marine detachments from shipboard police to military and political intervention ashore. Theodore Roosevelt's expansion of the Monroe Doctrine, particularly regarding the Panama Canal, led to an increased naval presence in the Caribbean region. In the first three decades of the twentieth century, seagoing Marines landed twenty-one times in Central America, Mexico, and the West Indies. Marine Captain John Thomason of the *Rochester* reminisced that his detachment was ". . . a splendid weapon, this guard: 103 Marines, 80 rifles, 2 machine guns, and the 37mm gun for landing force; it was an organization proved and competent and regarded with schooled respect by more than one frustrated Latin-American *junta*."

In the 1914 Annual Report of the Navy Department, the Marine Corps postulated, "It is of the utmost advantage to the naval service to have at its disposal a corps of officers and men who are trained equally well for service on board ships of the navy or on shore in landing operations." Congress agreed, and in an unprecedented move, authorized an increase in the Corps' strength by forty additional ships' detachments and an expeditionary battalion to handle the increased responsibilities.

On the opposite side of the world, Captain John Twiggs "Handsome Jack" Myers landed a seagoing contingent on the China coast in response to a threat to the International Settlement in Peking (now Beijing). A wave of antiforeign protests and escalating attacks led by the Righteous Harmony Society had reached a peak in 1900. Alternate translations such as "Righteous Harmonious Fists" and "Fists of Righteous Harmony" led to the society being called "Boxers" by Westerners, and the uprising became known as the "Boxer Rebellion." The U.S. presence in the Philippines won during the Spanish-American War gave the United States greater interest and power in the region. As "Handsome Jack" led his heavily armed contingent into Tienjin, the halfway mark on the way to Peking, Herbert Hoover, a young mining engineer and future president, recalled: "I do not remember a more satisfying musical performance than the bugles of the American Marines [sic] entering the settlement playing, 'There'll Be a Hot Time in the Old Town Tonight.'"

After the Philippines (1899–1902), seagoing Marines landed in rapid succession in Syria (1903), Abyssinia (1903–1904), Morocco (1904), Korea (1903–1904), and Turkey (1912). These forays were often conducted by combining Marine detachments from several ships, including sailors who were partially trained as naval infantry. The bluejackets were a willing crew—ready to fight—but sometimes left a lot to be desired while ashore. Captain "Fritz" Wise had an up-front and personal encounter with a naval landing party at Vera Cruz, Mexico. "I climbed up on the roof. As I stood there looking around, suddenly I heard bullets whizzing all around me. The plaster on the parapet flew on both sides of me. I flopped! From where I lay I could see a group of American sailors on the roof of a high building. Evidently they took me for a Mexican sniper. It was a miracle that I wasn't hit."

Super Dreadnought

A worldwide naval arms race in the first decade of the twentieth century caused great concern in Congress. America's economic strength lay in foreign commerce, which depended on a strong navy to maintain freedom of the seas. However, the United States was faced with threats on both coasts. The German ship-building program was in high gear, threatening the balance of power in the Atlantic. A 1911 intelligence report estimated that the U.S. Navy lagged behind Germany and was in danger of becoming a second-rank power. In the Pacific, Japan's lopsided victory over the Russian fleet at Tsushima in 1905 marked her as a formidable naval power. The victory seemed to demonstrate the superiority of big guns and big

ships, which blended in with America's tradition of heavy ships. The General Board, an influential naval advisory panel, added its weight. "The power of the fleet is measured by the number and efficiency of its . . . battleships."

As a result of these concerns, Congress, in 1913, increased its authorization to two Pennsylvania-class battleships. They were to be a new line of "super dreadnoughts" that fired a broadside heavier than any foreign battleship of the time. They were designed for a great naval battle in which two lines of capital ships steamed on parallel lines pounding each other with large-caliber shells, while destroyers darted out to fire torpedoes.

The thirty-three-thousand-ton Pennsylvania-class dreadnoughts were more than six hundred feet long, the length of two football fields, and one hundred feet wide. Their superstructure loomed a hundred feet over the harbor waters.

USS *Arizona* BB-39

When the decision was made public to build the ship, Arizona's political leaders successfully petitioned the secretary of the navy to name her after the youngest state. She was the third warship to bear the name. Construction started on March 16, 1914, at the New York Navy Yard, more popularly known as the Brooklyn Navy Yard.

The shipyard was located across from the Battery on the Brooklyn side of the East River in the Wallabout Basin, a semicircle bend of the East River. Established in 1801, it was one of the oldest government shipyards in the country and figured prominently in New York City's rich nautical history. Robert Fulton's first steamship, the *Fulton*, was built there in 1815 and the USS *Maine* in 1890. In 1871, Marines from the navy yard were ordered to restore order in "Irish Town," after the police and federal agents were thrown out of the area by the local toughs. Colonel Robert Debs Heinl wrote that "Brooklyn's Marines, under a hail of everything from pistol balls to brickbats, battled Brooklyn's Irish, while federal 'revenooers' smashed still after still."[2]

During the Spanish-American War, the 1st Marine Battalion was organized at the navy yard. Its fierce commander, Colonel Robert W. Huntington, a sixty-six-year-old Civil War veteran of Bull Run, marched the Marines through the streets of Brooklyn, to the cheers of the local citizenry. As their transport pulled away from the dock, the navy yard band played "The Girl I Left Behind Me."

The *Arizona* began to take shape when shipyard cranes lifted massive steel plates into place to form the

Marines practice scaling the
New York Navy Yard wall.
Defense Department 27
H-516488

The *Arizona* starts to take shape as the bottom and
sides of her hull are placed. *History Division, USMC*

Work begins on the internal structure of the *Arizona*.
History Division, USMC

keel. One hundred and fifty giant curved frames were
added, spaced at four-foot intervals to act as "ribs" to
support the skin of the ship. Decks and bulkheads followed, transforming the odd steel skeleton into the look
of a ship. The steel that went into the hull was laid out on
full-scale templates, cut to size and assembled in the
yard's shops before final installment on the skeleton. Six

thousand tons of armor plate were used in protecting
vital spaces. After more than a year, *Arizona* was ready to
be christened.

A special medal was struck commemorating the event
and presented to the official guests. It was purportedly
made of gunmetal recovered from the USS *Maine*. The
face of the medal was stamped *Arizona* in Greek letter-

ing, while the reverse bore the inscription, "USS *Arizona*, launched June 1915." An eighty-piece silver service, designed by Reed and Barton, was commissioned for presentation to the ship. Each piece was emblazoned with the Arizona coat of arms. Its ten-thousand-dollar price tag was paid for by individual citizens and the six largest mining companies in the state. (In 1940, prior to the *Arizona* sailing for Hawaii, the silver service was taken from the ship and placed in storage. It now resides in the capitol rotunda in Phoenix.)

A great celebration was planned. The Secretary of the Navy, Josephus Daniels, headed the Washington delegation, which included a congressman, two cabinet-level secretaries, and the little-known Assistant Secretary of the Navy, Franklin D. Roosevelt. Governor W. P. Hunt led the fifty-nine-member state committee. One of its members, Ms. Esther Ross of Prescott, was appointed by Hunt to christen the ship. The seventeen-year-old high school student was the daughter of a prominent Arizona citizen—and political confidant to the governor. On the eve of the ceremony, Ms. Ross was quoted as saying, "This is one of the greatest honors that ever could befall a girl. But it is my sincere wish that the vessel I am to christen will be used to keep the peace rather than make war." A quarter century later her prophetic comments foreshadowed a "Day of Infamy," instead of keeping the peace, *Arizona* symbolized the embodiment of wartime fervor.

The christening was the subject of some controversy. A June 18, 1915, edition of the *New York Review* heralded:

Bulkheads further define the below decks structure of the *Arizona*. History Division, USMC

"No Grape Juice Christening for Arizona."

The superdreadnought Arizona will be christened at New York tomorrow with champagne, and a bottle of water also will be broken over her bow for good measure.

The wine will be used to satisfy all those people who believe a warship is not a real warship unless it is christened with something stronger than water. The water will be used to satisfy the prohibitionists of the state.

But that is not all: the water which is to be used is from the Roosevelt dam, and a lot of the Bull Moose are insisting that nothing could be more

Traditions of the Sea

Early seafarers spoke of ships in the feminine gender because of the close dependence they had on them for life and sustenance. The Romans would dedicate a completed ship to a goddess, under whose protection she would sail. The ship often carried the deity's wooden image on her bow to aid in finding her way. In languages that use gender for common nouns—such as French and Spanish—the feminine form is used for boats, ships, and other vehicles. For example, the French word for boat is *la barque* and in Spanish it's *la barca* (*la* being feminine). Even in today's politically correct navy, old salts continue to use "she," as in "she's anchored in stream." One wag suggested that the term came about because, "If you don't treat them like a lady, they will act up and cause havoc."

Christening goes back five thousand years, when the Babylonians sacrificed oxen to the gods when a ship was completed. The U.S. Navy's first recorded christening was the USS *Constitution* on October 21, 1797, in Boston. Captain James Seve, her sponsor, broke a bottle of wine across Old Ironsides' bow. U.S. Navy ships were christened only by men until the nineteenth century. "Miss Watson" of Philadelphia was among the first women to christen a ship, the USS *Germantown* in 1846.

A huge crowd gathers in anticipation of the launching of the *Arizona* on June 19, 1915. *History Division, USMC*

calculated to make a battleship fight than to christen it with water from a dam that bears the name of the erstwhile colonel of the Rough Riders.

Governor Hunt of Arizona, who is here at the head of the State party on the way to christen the battleship, is a Democrat. The responsibility of deciding the christening was put up to him by the Navy Department.

Governor Hunt looked pained today when newspaper men pressed him with the question whether it was to be water or wine. He was inclined to talk about the hot weather, but finally admitted wine would be used.

"You know, we believe in punch in Arizona," said the Governor, "and many people in our state think the ship must be christened with something that has a punch to it."

Others of the party said that, while wine was to be used, a bottle of water would also be broken over the vessel to satisfy the Prohibitionists and the Bull Moosers."

The two christening bottles, one wrapped in copper bands from Arizona mines and the other encased in silver, were custom ordered from New York's Tiffany & Company.[3] Despite the controversy, the president of the New York State Women's Christian Temperance Movement promised that her organization would not interfere with the christening, "Neither protest, nor delegation will be made to Governor Hunt."

Special security precautions were implemented to handle the huge crowd that was expected to attend. The shipyard's Marine guard was turned out in force with orders to stop anyone from interrupting the ceremony. Patrols were increased around the yard's perimeter brick walls. Extra yard police were brought in to supplement the Marines. They were strategically placed around the VIP area and entranceways. Ticket holders were directed to enter through one of the four massive iron gateways, where they were screened by the yard police. Harbor craft were warned to stay close to the Manhattan shoreline an hour before and an hour after the christening.

Hours before the 1:00 p.m. ceremony, thousands of invited guests swarmed into a navy yard festooned with flags and bunting in honor of the occasion. A U.S. Navy band serenaded the crowd—estimated at fifty thousand to seventy-five thousand people, the largest to ever see an American ship launched—with patriotic music. It was a perfect spring day, blue cloudless sky, and warm temperature. The crowd was in a holiday mood, as the official party took its place on a raised wooden platform. The ceremony commenced with a brief prayer, followed by remarks by the various dignitaries. Finally, Ms. Ross rose and stepped close to the ship's bow where the two

Patriotic newspaper coverage of the *Arizona* launching.
History Division, USMC

LAUNCHING OF THE U. S. S. "ARIZONA," AT BROOKYN NAVY YARD, JUNE 19, 1915

The U. S. S. "Arizona," Uncle Sam's greatest fighting ship and sister to the great U. S. S. "Pennsylvania" which was recently launched, going down the ways in the presence of about 100,000 invited guests to the christening and launching of the mighty vessel.

Arizona slides out of the ways, the dock in which she was built, at New York Navy Yard, June 19, 1915. *History Division, USMC*

christening bottles hung suspended from ropes, wreathed in red, white, and blue ribbons. Ms. Ross grasped the bottles and swung them with all her might—she had practiced at home with syrup and barley bottles—and shouted, "I christen thee *Arizona*!" The wine bottle broke, however the water bottle stayed intact—avoiding the bad omen of christening a ship with water. Ms. Ross stepped back to be congratulated by the official party, amid the roar of the crowd.

Underneath the platform, hidden by the maze of timbers, an unknown shipyard employee pushed a hydraulic trigger, which released *Arizona*'s wooden cradle. Slowly at first, but with gathering speed, the ship slid stern first

Arizona slips free of her ways into the East River. Tug boats stand ready to move the unpowered ship to her berth. *History Division, USMC*

Arizona Construction Cost

The *Arizona* cost $9.8 million, or approximately $211 per ton, which according to the secretary of the navy represented a savings over that of preceding battleships. He credited the cost reductions to increased efficiencies at the Brooklyn Navy Yard, even though the navy was forced to pay bonuses for overtime work because of the scarcity of labor. The navy was involved in a scandal connected with bidding her armor plate. Three contractors submitted identical bids, to the penny, leaving no doubt of their collusion. In the past, the navy had assigned one-third of the quantity to each of the bidders—which allowed them to fix the price. In *Arizona*'s case, the navy rejected all bids and required the contractors to resubmit. In the next round, the low bidder came in $112,000 less than the original proposal.

down the ways, to the cheers of the vast throng. She plunged into the East River with a gigantic splash, sending waves cascading along the shore. Contemporary photos show the launch proceeding without a hitch, neither bottle—wine nor water—so much as scratched the red primer off her armored hull.

As yard tugs pushed *Arizona*'s hulk into her berth, the official party adjourned to the venerable Twenty-third Regiment Armory, Bedford and Atlantic Avenue, Brooklyn, for a lunch sponsored by the shipyard employees. There was no mention of whether alcoholic libations were served, nor if the rich and famous survived rubbing elbows with the hardscrabble workforce.

Service with the Fleet

The formation of bluejackets and Marines stood rigidly at attention as Captain John D. McDonald read the orders appointing him to command. He then ordered the National Ensign and the commissioning pennant hoisted. The ship's band broke into the "Star-Spangled Banner." The first entry in the ship's log recorded, "USS *Arizona* (BB-39) commissioned this date, October 16, 1916, Captain J. D. McDonald Commanding." With this simple ceremony, *Arizona* stood ready to join the fleet.

Months prior to the commissioning, skilled shipyard workers labored to complete fitting her out. It was a massive effort to transform the bare hull that Ms. Ross christened into a fully functional and habitable warship. Hundreds of thousands of man-hours were devoted to installing her systems; from the engine room to the mainmast, for every piece of equipment had to meet the navy's high standards of performance and acceptability.

During the fitting-out process, hundreds of sailors and Marines reported for duty. They ranged from grizzled

Marine Sergeant J. B. Marshall reporting for duty. *History Division, USMC*

A group of U.S. Navy petty officers and one Marine NCO, the sergeant standing at left. *Author's collection*

Crime and Punishment

DESERTED last night from the *Andrew Doria*, lying at Fort-Island, two marines, viz. THOMAS ROBINSON, an Irish-man, between thirty and forty years of age, about five feet seven inches high. THOMAS FURMAN, an Irishman, about thirty years of age, near five feet six inches high. They took away with them a small whaleboat, two or three great coats, and two watches, one of which is numbered 515, and maker's name Edward Vaughan, London. Whoever secures said deserters, so that I get them again, shall have Forty Dollars reward, and reasonable charges, or Twenty Dollars for either of them. THOMAS VAUGHAN, Lieut.[4]

If they were ever caught, Robinson and Furman would not have been treated with leniency. In 1776, a court-martial awarded Private Henry Hasson ". . . fifty Lashes for Desertion & twenty one Lashes for Quiting his Guard without leave of his Officers, on his bare back well laid on at the head of his Company." Thirty-nine years later, punishment remained harsh: "On Friday, 13 January 1815, the Marine Band, playing the 'Dead March' from *Saul*, escorted [the deserter] from the barracks at 8th and Eye Streets to Hospital Square, where he was stood up beside an open grave and shot in hollow square."

Flogging continued to be widely used to maintain discipline. The culprit was escorted in front of his assembled shipmates to the place of punishment. His shirt was stripped, baring his back. His wrists and ankles were made fast, stretching his arms over his head. The chief boatswain held a green baize bag, from which he drew out a cat-o'nine-tails. The "cat" consisted of nine white pieces of cord about twenty inches long fixed into a wooden handle. Three knots were tied into each strand. When all was ready, the captain ordered the boatswain, "Do your duty," and the punishment began. An eyewitness described a flogging: "The shrieks of the youngster were dreadful. He called upon God and the holy angels to save him. After the first dozen, he fainted and hung by his wrists." Flogging was finally abolished by Congress in 1862.

chief petty officers and "Old Corps" noncommissioned officers to pink-cheeked apprentice seamen and recruits right out of boot camp. Seaman Oree Weller vividly remembered reporting aboard *Arizona*. "A rag-tag lot we were as we went aboard. We stuck out like sore thumbs, with our high-topped shoes and long white trousers. Those made us dead giveaways as boots, and we had to take the consequences." The "old salts," the backbone of the battleship navy and Marine Corps, took the young-sters in tow and molded them into an effective team.

Arizona heads down New York's East River on her maiden voyage, November 16, 1916. *History Division, USMC*

Their methods were as varied as their personalities—but it was the mark of the times that their rule was law—the system did not tolerate disobedience or slackers. Those who didn't learn the harsh realities of service life ran afoul of "Rocks and Shoals," the Articles for Government of the Navy. In the early days of the Republic, Marine

Anchored in Guantanamo Bay, Cuba. Note the awning in the stern to provide relief from the sun. *History Division, USMC*

discipline was simple and severe (see "Crime and Punishment" sidebar p. 36). In Private Kalinowski's day, a common sentence included a stay in the brig on "piss and punk" (bread and water).

A month after taking command, Captain McDonald watched as the Manila hawsers fell away, freeing *Arizona* from the pier. At that moment, the National Ensign was run up the mainmast and the navy jack struck below. Dockyard workers waved in tribute to their work as the tug eased the warship into the current. The deck vibrated with the raw power of her 35,000-horsepower turbine engines as the *Arizona* eased down the East River to the Atlantic for

a shakedown cruise to Guantanamo Bay, Cuba, via the Virginia Capes. She passed under the towering concrete monuments of the city. Hundreds of New Yorkers thronged the Brooklyn and Manhattan bridge walkways, anxious for a glimpse of the great ship as she passed under the roadways. Her masts majestically glided underneath, almost within reach of the enthusiastic crowd. Crewmen on the upper decks kept a wary eye out for going-away mementos that were dropped by an overzealous observer—a silver dollar at that height was deadly. As she reached the mouth of the harbor, another lady appeared on the starboard side. Even hardened old salts stopped work to watch the Statue of Liberty glide past.

Arizona anchored in Guantanamo Bay. The crew was allowed ashore for a short liberty but soon found that the naval base was a hot, windy, barren place with little to do but gather around the local canteen. The youngsters

Arizona operated out of Guantanamo Bay for the first few months of 1920. The bow has an awning as well. *History Division, USMC*

quickly found out that Caribbean delights did not include wine, women, and song. Most were happy to return to the ship and escape the brutally hot sun. After bidding a fond farewell to the tropical scene, the ship sailed north to test fire her main and secondary batteries. Seaman L. C. Perdue remembered the big guns. "It was like being in the middle of an exploding munitions factory. The noise and concussion smacks you in the face. You pull your cap down on your head as tight as you can. Your ears are packed with cotton. You stand on your tiptoes to cushion the shock—and you open your mouth to relieve the pressure on your ears. Then all hell breaks loose!" The first salvo was such a terrific blast that it buckled several bulkheads, which had to be repaired at the navy yard.

On December 24, she returned to the navy yard for a post shakedown overhaul. The crew enjoyed the holidays in the "Big Apple," while shipyard workers corrected deficiencies. Three months later, *Arizona* sailed from Brooklyn to join Battleship Division 8 at Norfolk. That same day, President Woodrow Wilson appeared before Congress to request a formal declaration of war against Germany. His words, "Keep the world safe for democracy," rang out, to thunderous applause. Later, Wilson wept because, he said, "My message today was a message of death for our young men."

The navy immediately went on a war footing. *Arizona* was ordered to patrol the East Coast to counter Germany's U-Boat threat—the U-53 had torpedoed a British merchantman off Nantucket Island some months before.

Stern view, port side, April 3, 1917, as *Arizona* leaves New York for Norfolk. *History Division, USMC*

To ease fears of a German attack, Franklin Roosevelt wrote a tongue-in-cheek letter to his wife poking fun at the building panic. "I meant to tell you that if by any perfectly wild chance a German submarine should come into the bay and start to shell Eastport [Maine] or the Pool, I want you to grab the children and beat it into the woods!"

Arizona's bluejackets were anxious to get into the fight, but her boilers burned fuel oil, which was in short supply in Great Britain, at a prodigious rate. So, while one division of coal-burning battleships was sent to reinforce the British Grand Fleet against the German High Seas Fleet, *Arizona* spent the war in American home waters indoctrinating and training new seamen. Many of her experienced seamen left to join the newly expanded fleet, resulting in a crew that consisted of a great many transients, who were reassigned as soon as they were trained. Endless drills conditioned the new men to accomplish tasks without thinking, a necessary requirement in war time.

A week after the Armistice was signed, *Arizona* rendezvoused with the transport *George Washington*, which

Arizona at sea. *National Archives 80 G 32545*

was carrying President Wilson to the Paris Peace Conference. Together with her battleship division, *Arizona* served as the honor escort for the president as he arrived in Brest, France, on December 13, 1918. The crew "manned the rails" as the president's ship steamed past. The ship fired a twenty-one-gun salute, while the crew gave three cheers. The crew enjoyed a short liberty before returning to the United States.

Four months later, she returned to the continent in response to an emergency at the port of Smyrna, Turkey. Greek forces were battling Turkish nationals for control of the city. Upon arrival, *Arizona*'s heavily armed Marine detachment hurried ashore to guard the American consulate. They took up defensive positions around the building, in a show of force that discouraged hostile actions. The detachment also provided escort to the ship for American citizens caught up in the violence. By June, the situation had stabilized and *Arizona* sailed for home.

For the next several years, she cruised up and down the Atlantic coast of the United States and the Caribbean "showing the flag" and protecting American interests in

Above: *Arizona* passes through the Panama Canal on her way home for a major refit. Her original cage masts would be replaced with tripod masts. *History Division, USMC*

Opposite: *Arizona* with newly installed fore and aft tripod masts. *History Division, USMC*

the Banana Republics of Central America. Beginning in 1921, *Arizona* was transferred to the Pacific, home-ported in San Pedro, California, and became part of the Battle Fleet. She served variously as flagship for Battle-ship Divisions 2, 3, and 4 while participating in a succession of fleet training exercises, ranging from the Caribbean, Central America, Canal Zone, Hawaii, and the West Coast of the United States. While in Washington's Puget Sound area, *Arizona*'s landing force conducted maneuvers. The ship carried a small 3-inch fieldpiece, which was manhandled ashore from a whale-boat. The combined force of Marines and sailors staged mock battles. One of the seamen related how he slacked off. "I was very good at dying quick. As soon as I found a convenient shade tree, I simulated being shot, so I could take it easy for the remainder of the battle."

Following Fleet Problem IX, a large-scale training maneuver staged by the navy in 1929, *Arizona* transited the Panama Canal and sailed to Norfolk, Virginia, for a year-long period of modernization. During the long hours on duty, a Marine orderly amused himself by teaching the captain's parrot to repeat a risqué expression. The captain's wife was not amused, and the orderly enjoyed a three-day vacation in the brig, sampling the cook's bread and drinking ship's water. The overhaul completely transformed *Arizona*. Her armament was updated with eight new 5-inch 25-caliber antiaircraft guns, replacing the outdated 3-inch mounts. Her main battery was given an extra 15 degrees of elevation, doubling her range to twenty miles, and the 5-inch 51-caliber broadside guns were moved up one level to the main deck. New fore and aft tripod masts replaced the old cage types, and extra armor was added below the upper decks, as a counter to the emerging air threat. Extra compartments, called "blisters," were added to the side of the hull to increase the ship's protection against torpedo attack. The submerged torpedo tubes were removed and the space compartmentalized to increase watertight integrity.

Finally, the engines were upgraded, allowing the ship to maintain a twenty-one-knot speed.

Arizona had barely cleared the yard when sailing orders arrived. She was directed to transport President Herbert Hoover on a ten-day inspection cruise to Puerto Rico and St. Thomas in the Virgin Islands. Under the eagle-eyed supervision of the petty officers and noncommissioned officer, the crew turned to with a vengeance. The engine room was painted, as was the black boot stripe along the waterline. Round after round of inspections ensured that the vessel was shipshape—her brightwork gleamed, the teak decks were holystoned to a brilliant white, and her upper works glowed with fresh paint—and her crew fairly shined, with fresh haircuts and clean clothes.

Security was increased with additional Marines. Lieutenant Joseph C. Burger was aboard the USS *Utah* when the navy decommissioned her. "It was decided the Marine detachment would board the USS *Arizona*[, which] was just completing modernization. We received orders to take the President on a cruise to Puerto Rico and the Caribbean." Armed security posts were established

Above: President Hoover's flag flying from the top of the mainmast. Note the church pennant flying from the halyard. It is the only pennant that flies above the National Ensign. The range clock on the mast is a gunnery device. *National Archives 80-G-461026*

Left: President Hoover meeting *Arizona*'s officers. Note the ship's aircraft atop the aft turrets. *History Division, USMC*

President Hoover inspecting *Arizona*'s crew. Note the Marine detachment at "present arms" in the background. *History Division, USMC*

Arizona at sea. President Hoover's flag flies from the mainmast. *National Archives 80-G-461035*

Hoover taking a stroll on the quarterdeck. Note the Marine, at right, making sure the deck is clear for the president. *History Division, USMC*

around the flag quarters (the presidential area), with orders to "allow no unauthorized person to enter the area . . . and detain unauthorized individuals who attempt to enter." The detachment commander hand-picked several Marines to serve as Hoover's orderlies while he was aboard.

President Hoover boarded a train at Union Station for the overnight trip to Norfolk. Upon arrival at the naval base, the president and his official party boarded the admiral's barge for the short ride to the *Arizona*. A bitterly cold wind blew across the harbor, producing a chop that threatened to overwhelm several of the party's more delicate stomachs. As the president gained the quarterdeck, the *Arizona*'s official party rendered honors. In a concession to the freezing weather, the eight "side boys" and the bugler were allowed to wear heavy woolen P-coats and watch caps.

Formal picture of President Hoover, seated front and center, with *Arizona*'s crew. *History Division, USMC*

The captain welcomed President Hoover to the ship and shepherded him on a quick tour of the upper deck and bridge before showing him to his cabin. Within hours *Arizona* was under way for southern waters, and President Hoover inspected the ship's crew. After his initial inspection, the president showed little interest in the crew. During his regular morning constitutionals, a Marine sergeant was assigned to keep the decks clear of all crewmembers.

Seaman James Lawson didn't like the idea of senior officers getting special treatment. "It didn't make any difference if you had work to do. If we were cleaning the guns, for example, we had to quit cleaning the guns if the Admiral was going to take a walk. A Marine would come

by and say, 'The admiral is going for his walk. Clear the deck.' We'd go back into the turret till it was all clear." Before leaving the ship at Hampton Roads, Hoover consented to have his picture taken with the crew.

In the summer of 1931, *Arizona* transited the Panama Canal and returned to San Pedro, California, where she continued to be home-ported for the next decade, operating with the Battle Force (previously the Battle Fleet, renamed after a 1930 reorganization) off the coast of California and in northern Pacific waters. She became something of a celebrity in 1934, when the navy agreed to allow a film company to use her in the romantic comedy *Here Comes the Navy*, starring James Cagney and Pat O'Brien. The ship received great exposure because the film was a huge success, even being nominated for Best Picture.

On Tuesday, April 2, 1940, the balance of the Battle Force sailed from West Coast ports for the Hawaiian Operating Area, joining its Hawaiian detachment—eight heavy cruisers, one aircraft carrier, and sixteen destroyers stationed at Pearl Harbor in 1939—to carry out Fleet Problem XXI. The fleet was to remain in the Hawaiian waters until Thursday, May 9, and then return to the West Coast on or about May 17. Less than a week before the exercise ended, Admiral Richardson received a classified message directing him to remain on station for an indeterminate time because "of the deterrent effect which it is thought your presence may have on the Japs going into the East Indies."

Arizona at anchor off San Pedro, California, 1935. *History Division, USMC*

Arizona on maneuvers around the time of its reassignment to Pearl Harbor. Note the planes in the upper left. *History Division, USMC*

CHAPTER THREE

THE HAWAIIAN OPERATION

"The rise and fall of the Empire depends upon this battle. Every man is expected to do his utmost."
—Admiral Isoroku Yamamoto
Commander in Chief of the Japanese Combined Fleet

As relations with Japan worsened in the summer of 1940, President Roosevelt remained convinced that permanently transferring the Battle Force to Pearl Harbor would act as "a restraining influence." The U.S. government did not want the Japanese advancing into Southeast Asia, within striking distance of the Philippines, which had been U.S. territory since the Spanish-American War and a U.S. commonwealth since 1935.

The fleet transfer was strongly opposed by Admiral James O. Richardson, its commander in chief. Richardson had been personally selected by President Roosevelt over several more senior officers, but Richardson was no political appointee. He spoke candidly, with great force on those issues in which he believed. He did not believe that positioning the fleet in Hawaii would restrain the Japanese. In fact, he thought just the opposite, that the fleet would be at a serious disadvantage.

Richardson had two face-to-face meetings with the president, on July 8 and October 8, 1940, to voice his concerns. During the October meeting, which Richardson characterized as "waxing hot and heavy," he expressed frustration with the president's order. "Mr. President, I feel I must tell you that senior officers of the Navy do not have the trust and confidence in the civilian leadership of this country that is essential for the successful prosecution of a war in the Pacific." In the president's mind, Richardson had clearly overstepped his

bounds as a serving officer and three months later, he relieved him. The secretary of the navy told him that he was relieved because he "hurt the President's feelings." The fleet remained at Pearl Harbor.

After being relieved from command, Richardson maintained a stoic public silence regarding the incident. He was described as a big man, courtly and courteous—a gentleman of the old school—a man of high moral principles. He never criticized Roosevelt and even went so far as to burn his diary, fearing that some of his observations might hurt others. In 1945, he appeared before the Congressional Pearl Harbor Investigation Committee. At the conclusion of his testimony, he said, "I never bore any resentment toward President Roosevelt because of my detachment. . . . He was the constitutional commander in chief [and] I was one of his senior subordinates; there was a difference of opinion; each of us frankly expressed his views; neither could induce the other to change his opinion; I was relieved of command. . . ."

Marine Major General Wilburt S. Brown was a captain aboard the *Pennsylvania* at the time of the fleet's transfer. "Roosevelt hit upon the idea of threatening Japan with an empty gun. For some reason he thought he was cowing the Japanese by keeping the fleet out there. The Japanese knew readiness for war much better than he did." Roosevelt's decision played right into their hands. In late summer 1940, Admiral Isoroku

Pearl Harbor in 1937, looking much as it would to Japanese pilots four years later. Merry Point and the submarine base are at left near the oil tank farm. Battleships are moored throughout the harbor and alongside Ford Island. Compare to the photograph below, taken about five weeks before the attack. *National Archives 80-G-451160*

Yamamoto, commander in chief of the Japanese Combined Fleet, devised a plan to destroy the U.S. fleet in the Pacific at the onset of war—a surprise attack on Pearl Harbor.

The Gibraltar of the Pacific

Pearl Harbor's strategic significance lay in its value as the westernmost outpost of defense from Japanese threats against American security interests in the Pacific and, in case of war, a springboard for offensive operations against Japan. As early as 1909, the navy decided to make Pearl Harbor a major base, but it was not until after World War I that construction moved into high gear when the secretary of the navy recommended that "a first-class naval base, complete in all respects, capable of taking care of the whole fleet, be developed in the Hawaiian Islands as a strategic necessity.... Pearl Harbor should be immediately developed as a first-class Naval Base."

Thirty million dollars was allocated for a five-year building program to upgrade and expand the harbor's

Pearl Harbor overview, October 30, 1941. *National Archives 80-G-182874*

Ford Island in the 1940s, looking southeast toward Hickam Field, its triangle of runways visible in the upper center. The sunken *Arizona* and capsized *Oklahoma* are visible on the far side of the island; the capsized training ship *Utah* is on the near side. *History Division, USMC*

yards, docks, and other support facilities. The largest project, dredging the main channel, continued in stages for the next thirty years, until even the largest fleet aircraft carriers could enter the harbor with ease. Only a single channel into and out of the harbor remained, however, presenting the constant danger of blockage. Despite the emphasis on construction, one of the first tenants, a submarine flotilla, had to clear the land and construct its own administration building, mess hall, and service shops.

Ford Island, a 450-acre site in the middle of Pearl Harbor, was purchased in 1918 for a joint army-navy seaplane field. The Army's 6th Aero Squadron took up residence immediately, followed by the navy's contingent of four seaplanes and forty-nine men a year later. In 1923, the navy took over sole occupancy and established a permanent air station that consisted of a four-thousand-foot runway, concrete wharf, seaplane hangars, and administrative buildings.

Pearl Harbor Navy Yard looking west. An aircraft carrier is moored along Ford Island at upper right, and three seaplanes are in the channel just off the tip of the island. *National Archives 80-G-451121*

During the 1920s and 1930s, Pearl Harbor and the surrounding area were transformed. Ship and aircraft repair facilities were constructed; fuel storage tanks were added and a series of forts constructed along Oahu's coast for defense of the island. By 1938, the navy yard occupied 498 acres and included one battleship drydock with its supporting industrial establishment, a marine railway, administrative offices, two above-ground fuel-oil tank farms, supply depot, and housing—a total of 190 buildings. Periodic fleet exercises tested the defenses. During the 1932 and 1938 exercises, navy carrier–based aircraft penetrated the island's defenses, demonstrating the vulnerability of the fleet anchorage. However, a journalist, with implicit army and navy approval, wrote that an attack from carrier-based airplanes was improbable because of the island's defenses. The administration considered the island of Oahu "the strongest fortress in the world."

Navy Yard looking southwest. Note the ship channel in the upper center of the photo. *National Archives 80-G-451123*

In Harm's Way

On February 1, 1941, Admiral Richardson was replaced by Admiral Husband E. Kimmel in a change of command ceremony aboard the USS *Pennsylvania*, flagship of the renamed Pacific Fleet.

Kimmel was a "relatively young rear admiral, who had been advanced over some forty senior officers." He was considered a hard-driving officer, fiercely devoted to

Rear Admiral Husband Kimmel, circa later 1930s. *Naval Historical Center NH 54303*

Captain Isaac C. Kidd, USN, circa 1939, Commanding Officer USS *Arizona*. *Naval Historical Center NH 97385*

duty. He insisted on order, routine, and efficiency. As a ship handler, woe be it to the man who did not execute a command crisply, mix up a signal, or blow a maneuver. He did not suffer fools well and could fly off the handle at the drop of a hat. In fact, he was known to fling it on the deck and stamp on it in a fit of anger. Despite this personality quirk, Kimmel inspired a strong devotion among his staff. Colonel Omar T. Pfeiffer worked closely with Kimmel. "He instilled in me a loyalty that nothing could shake and to this day never has been shaken." Even his enemies gave him credit. Admiral Yamamoto said of him, "Admiral Kimmel, himself a young man, is said to have gone up to be commander in chief by his ability. He is a man with much courage and guts."

Rear Admiral Isaac Campbell Kidd, commander of the First Battleship Division (*Arizona*, *Nevada*, and *Pennsylvania*) was among the sixteen flag officers in attendance at the change of command. Forty-six-year-old Isaac Kidd was an experienced battleship sailor. He served four previous tours in dreadnoughts, including eighteen months as commanding officer of the *Arizona*.

Seaman Second Class William Goshen remembered him well. "Kidd was always around. He was very nice. He'd stop and talk to you just like he'd known you all his life. He had been the *Arizona*'s captain, and then he went back to school—war school in Washington—and when he came out he came back to the *Arizona* as admiral." Seaman Glenn Ballard recalled Kidd as "a physical nut. I remember he was death on drinking or getting in trouble. He was a stickler and known to slap a man in the brig for disorderly conduct." Twenty-three-year-old Private Russell J. McCurdy was the admiral's orderly. "We were from the Midwest and we would often talk about our hometowns, as friends, but on official orderly duty, I would stand at parade rest six feet from him. Admiral Kimmel was a firm believer in physical fitness. In the morning, we would work out doing rowing exercises."

The captain of the USS *Arizona*, Franklin Van Valkenburgh, was also at the change of command ceremony. Tall and white-haired, Van Valkenburgh was considered by some of the sailors to be a "gentleman of the old school." Like Kidd, he was a graduate of the U.S. Naval

Fleet anchorage, Pearl Harbor, 1941. At least seven battleships and one aircraft carrier are moored along Ford Island. *History Division, USMC*

Academy and a veteran battleship sailor. He had assumed command of the *Arizona* in February 1941. He was planning on retiring and remarked on more than one occasion how thrilled he was to be in command of a battleship at the end of his naval career.

As relations between the United States and Japan continued to deteriorate in spring 1941, Fleet training took on a new urgency. Kimmel divided his ships into three task forces, keeping one and sometimes two at sea. Captain Robert Cushman, commanding officer of *Pennsylvania*'s Marine detachment, recalled, "We trained. We went out to sea two weeks and back in one. Out at sea we trained night and day under war-time conditions—general quarters, blackened ship, and all the rest of it—one exercise after another. There was a sense that we were going to be in it [war]." Newspapers in Honolulu bannered, "It's going to happen this weekend. War is going to

American Intelligence Efforts

Unknown to the Japanese, American intelligence experts had broken their diplomatic code. A team of codebreakers painstakingly constructed a machine that duplicated the Japanese apparatus, Alphabetical Typewriter, Type 97, *shiki O-bum in-ji-ki*. The Japanese were convinced their code could not be broken. However, from the summer of 1940 on, the United States was reading virtually all the traffic between Tokyo and its important embassies. General George C. Marshall, army chief of staff, called this priceless asset "the most complete and up-to-the-minute intelligence that any nation had ever had concerning a probable enemy." The decoded transcripts were called *magic*. The decoding machine was a very closely held secret, and only the most senior government and military leaders knew of its existence. Admiral Kimmel was not one of those entrusted with the secret.

Admiral Isoroku Yamamoto, Japanese Navy. *Naval Historical Center NH 63430*

start." Captain Jack Earle remembered leaving Pearl Harbor on a "war-time footing, crew at general quarters, ammunition positioned; guns manned and ready. We were prepared for antisubmarine warfare defense."

The Japanese were closely watching the fleet. Kohichi Seki, a Japanese Consulate official closely monitored Pearl Harbor and reported, "Apparently the fleet goes to sea for a week of training and stays in Pearl Harbor one week. Every Wednesday, those at sea and those in the harbor change places." The local newspapers did not help security when it published a weekly fleet schedule. One front page headline trumpeted, "MAIN BODY OF FLEET TO SEA." Seki also noted the large number of ships in the harbor on Saturdays and Sundays.

At the end of March 1941, Ensign Takeo Yoshikawa, a trained naval intelligence agent, slipped into the islands to spy on the fleet. He was soon sending reports on its strength and composition. In late September, he received a "strictly secret" request from Japanese Naval Intelligence to report the disposition of ships in what amounted to a bomb grid of Pearl Harbor. The U.S. Navy intercepted and translated the message, which became known as the "bomb plot," but failed to recognize its significance.

On Saturday, December 6, President Roosevelt received a decoded message from Tokyo to its ambassador in the United States suspending further peace negotiations. Roosevelt exclaimed, "This means war." Unfortunately, U.S. code-breaking efforts could not determine where the Japanese would strike. Three hours and fifteen minutes after receiving the message, the Japanese launched its attack on Pearl Harbor.

Japanese Attack Plans

Admiral Isoroku Yamamoto, the fifty-seven-year-old commander of the Combined Fleet, sat in his cabin aboard the flagship *Nagato* waiting for word of the Pearl Harbor attack, a strike which he had masterminded. "We have no hope of winning a war against America," he wrote, "unless the United States fleet in Hawaiian waters can be destroyed." Yamamoto knew that his country could not fight a defensive war against the overwhelming military might of the United States; Japan must launch a devastating first strike.

In January 1941, Yamamoto directed his staff to study the feasibility of an attack against Pearl Harbor. By mid-April the study was complete and ready for the preparation of detailed plans by Combined Fleet staff officers. It was given the code designation "Operation AMO," but was more commonly known as the "Hawaiian Operation." As the plan moved from conception to implementation, Yamamoto held a series of tabletop exercises to test its validity. He quickly found that unless it was carried out in absolute secrecy, the attack force would sustain unacceptable losses. The exercise also revealed that he needed all of the navy's large aircraft carriers.

Yamamoto was forced to seek approval for the attack from the navy's top leadership, the Naval General Staff (NGS), which was strongly opposed to it. Operation AMO's offensive strategy represented a radical departure from the General Staff's firmly imbued philosophy of "The Great All-Out Battle (*Zengen Sakusen*)," in which the U.S. Navy would be lured across the Pacific, whittled down by submarines on the way, and, once in the waters near Japan, soundly defeated. The internal controversy raged until Yamamoto dug in his heels. "So long as I'm CinC [commander in chief], we shall go forward with the Hawaiian raid." The NGS backed off but tried to scuttle the plan by denying Yamamoto's request for six aircraft carriers. As before, Yamamoto did not hesitate to intervene. He threatened to resign, along with his entire staff, if his plan was not approved, in toto. His reputation and prestige was so great, the General Staff had to acquiesce.

The planners had to overcome other major problems. The first dealt with aircraft torpedoes. The Japanese did not have one that could be used in Pearl Harbor's shallow forty-five-foot depth. The problem was resolved by October, just in the nick of time, by the navy's torpedo experts, who added wooden fins and altered the aiming devices. However, only thirty torpedoes of the upgraded models would be available by mid-October, with another fifty at the end of the month, not enough to use for live training. Instead, the pilots substituted extensive training with dummy torpedoes against a stationary target the size of a *California*-type battleship to refine their dropping techniques. They learned that a slow speed (one hundred knots) and low altitude (fifty to sixty-five feet) was critical to achieve acceptable results. However, this tactic left them extremely vulnerable to antiaircraft fire, but it was the only viable option. Lieutenant Jinichi Goto was concerned. "We were shocked to hear about it. To us it sounded senseless and we did not think we could do it.... In the beginning I was very nervous ... but after a while I got used to it."

A second issue involved bombs. Extensive tests on various types and thicknesses of armor determined that Japan's existing inventory of bombs was not powerful enough to penetrate the armored deck of an American battleship. The test results indicated that almost a ton of high explosive was needed. The Japanese did not have the time or the material to make a new bomb, so they resolved the issue by modifying the *Nagato*-class battleship's 16-inch shells. The reconfigured bomb measured eight feet in length and weighed 800 kilograms (1,760 pounds).

A midget submarine beached on a coral reef at Waimanalo Bay on the northern side of Oahu on December 8. Ensign Kazuo Sakamaki was captured, becoming the United States' first Japanese prisoner of World War II. *National Archives 80-G-824567*

Because of the size and complexity of the operation, the Japanese grouped all their aircraft under one commander, a change from standard procedure. Commander Minoru Genda, an aviation pioneer, was picked to be the fleet's "air boss." He was considered a brilliant tactician and was given responsibility for devising the aviation attack plan. Genda, in turn, selected Lieutenant Commander Mitsuo Fuchida, a dynamic leader, to hammer the hundreds of air crew into a finely tuned, disciplined force. The two formed a unique team, which overcame the many obstacles placed in their path.

A final issue had to be resolved. The initial plan called for a major force of submarines to be in position to interdict and attack any vessels trying to escape from Pearl Harbor. Twenty large I-type submarines (*Sensuikan*) were to be deployed around the island of Oahu by December 6. They presented a formidable screen, capable of inflicting great damage on the fleeing American ships. At the last moment, five midget submarines (*Ko-hyotaki*) were added to the attack force. The two-man midgets were designed to operate against ships in enemy harbors. The seventy-eight-foot submersibles were powered by electric motors that propelled them at speeds up to twenty knots for short distances. They were armed with two 18-inch oxygen-fueled torpedoes that had great range, speed, and explosive power.

The midget submarines were assigned to penetrate the harbor and launch their torpedoes in the confusion of the air attack. They were to be carried to a position ten nautical miles off the mouth of Pearl Harbor on five specially configured I-class boats. Shortly after midnight, they were to be released to slink past the American patrol boats, navigate the narrow entrance past the antisubmarine net, and slip into the harbor. Fuchida hit the roof. He thought they added an unacceptable risk to the operation. Should they be discovered, the element of surprise would be lost. Yamamoto, however, was unconvinced and kept them in the plan.

In late November the plans were complete, and the *Kido Butai* (mobile striking force) was secretly assembled in the Kuriles. On November 23, Vice Admiral Chuichi Nagumo, its commander, opened a meeting of all his officers with, "Our mission is to attack Pearl Harbor!" His audience buzzed with excitement—this was the first time most of them knew of the daring plan. "No greater honor could we have as warriors," he exclaimed. With that exhortation, Nagumo turned the meeting over to his staff officers for detailed operational briefs. When the conference ended,

Admiral Chuichi Nagumo, Japanese Navy. *Naval Historical Center NH 63423*

the attendees stood and, in a burst of patriotic fervor, toasted the emperor, shouting "*Banzai, Banzai, Banzai.*"

That afternoon, Genda gathered all the pilots and gave them an overview of the operation. He began by informing them that the carriers would launch two waves of 350 aircraft, approximately 230 miles north of Pearl Harbor. The first wave of 183 aircraft would take off thirty minutes before sunrise, which would put them over Pearl Harbor at 0800. He pointed to Fuchida and said that he would direct the assembly of the first wave—high-level bombers at nearly ten thousand feet, torpedo bombers on the right at just over nine thousand feet, and dive bombers on the left at over eleven thousand feet—and lead it to the target. Upon reaching the target area, 45 fighters would break from the formation and eliminate the American air threat. In addition, 54 fighters, organized in groups of 18, would provide continuous security over the fleet. The second wave, 170 planes, would follow one hour later.

Japanese "Zero" fighter leaves *Akagi* on its way to attack Pearl Harbor, December 7, 1941. *National Archives 80-G-182252*

Japanese "Kate" carrier attack plane takes off from the aircraft carrier *Akagi*, circa March–April 1942. *National Archives 80-G-182245*

Fuchida took over to cover the air scheme in more detail. First, he divided them into tactical groups—Nakajima B5N2 "Kate" torpedo and horizontal bombers, Aichi D3A1 Type 99 "Val" dive bombers, and Mitsubishi A6M2 Type 00 "Zero" fighters—to review specific assignments. He used a model of Pearl Harbor and a series of his own hand-drawn sketches to illustrate the brief and to help the pilots visualize their targets. The mockup was remarkably detailed, down to individual

buildings and models of each American ship (a petty officer aboard the *Nagato* had carved them to scale). They were placed on the model according to the latest information from Japan's man in Hawaii, Ensign Takeo Yoshikawa. The pilots were so well briefed according to Genda that "on the day of the raid, it was so cloudy that only a small part of the island could be seen. A pilot caught sight of a small patch of land . . . and could immediately choose the right flying course."

As each group gathered around the table, Fuchida walked them through the attack. He started with the fighters. Once they reached the northern tip of Oahu, Fuchida would fire a rocket, releasing them to attack American aircraft both in the air and on the ground. The torpedo bombers, taking advantage of surprise, would sneak in at low altitude and attack the capital ships. As they came off the target, high-level bombers would then hit them with armor-piercing bombs. Finally, the dive bombers would administer the *coup de grâce*. The mix of weapons platforms—low, mid level, and high level—was designed to overwhelm any American defense with concentrated firepower.

Fuchida urged every pilot to press the attack, particularly the torpedo bombers. At one point he suggested that it might be necessary for them to launch suicide attacks if antitorpedo nets protected the battleships. "The first plane will make a charge route for the following planes," meaning that the first plane would crash the net to make a hole for succeeding aircraft. The series of briefings continued for two days, until every pilot could identify his target and how to attack it. Admiral Nagumo wrapped up with an exhortation, "This Task Force will attack and destroy the United States Fleet!"

Uncharted Waters

As dawn broke on a cold dank morning in Hitokappu Bay, Vice Admiral Nagumo gave the order to weigh anchor. Blinker signals pierced the semi-darkness. Signalmen relayed the deciphered flashes of light to the waiting commanders of the First Air Fleet. Within minutes the "Kido Butai" was making preparations for getting under way. At 0900, Tokyo time, the force slipped out of the isolated, fog-shrouded bay and headed eastward into the stormy North Pacific on its historic mission.

Admiral Nagumo had issued detailed sailing orders. The documents, several inches thick, prescribed the myriad operational details for the tactical disposition of the task force. They covered every possible contingency. First

Pearl Harbor chart found in Ensign Sakamaki's midget sub. *National Archives 80-G-413507*

and foremost, his fleet had to be able to fight. As the ships cleared the bay, they immediately took station in the fleet's tactical formation. The light cruiser *Abukuma* and four *Kagero*-class destroyers formed the frontal screen, followed by heavy cruisers *Tone* and *Chikuma*. Other destroyers guarded the flanks. The high-value vessels steamed within this protective umbrella; aircraft carriers in two parallel columns—starboard *Akagi*, *Kaga*, and *Shokaku*—port *Soryu*, *Hiryu*, and *Zaikaku*—followed by the precious tankers. Two battleships, *Kirishima* and *Hiei*, brought up the rear. Nagumo believed this formation offered the greatest flexibility and provided all-around security in case of attack. However, Vice Admiral Gunichi Mikawa, commander of the support force, was concerned. "With just two battleships and two cruisers, I was operating with no margin of security at all. I feared interception at sea and possible surface action—perhaps a running fight to the target—and I was convinced that my four ships would be inadequate to protect our carriers in case the U.S. Fleet closed in."

Nagumo carried an awesome responsibility. His fleet was sailing into uncharted waters, tactically and psychologically. The Japanese navy had always envisioned a defensive strategy, only engaging the American fleet in a climactic battle when it had tactical advantage. Now it was taking the fight to the Americans, and many of the senior naval leadership thought the mission was foolhardy. At one point, Yamamoto even threatened to resign if the attack on Pearl Harbor was not approved. Finally, the First Air Fleet was nothing short of a revolution in strategic thinking. It grouped three carrier divisions and their escorts under one commander, representing the cream of Japanese naval aviation. If the attack on Pearl Harbor failed and the fleet was destroyed, Japan would suffer a tremendous psychological blow. Nagumo, in the spirit of a samurai, kept a loaded .38-caliber pistol in his desk drawer in case of failure.

The attack had to be carried out in secret, which meant that the Japanese had to frustrate American efforts to track the fleet's radio transmissions. They went to extraordinary efforts. Nagumo imposed strict radio silence on his ships. To ensure his order was carried out, fuses were removed from all the radio transmitters, keying equipment was detached, and paper slips were placed in the keying mechanisms to prevent electrical contact. He ordered that all communications between ships were to be made by blinker and signal flags. As an additional security measure, the fleet changed their radio call signs, which caused American intelligence officers to inaccurately report Japanese ship locations. The deception was so good that Admiral Kimmel's intelligence officer lost track of the Japanese aircraft carriers. When Kimmel was briefed on December 2, he exclaimed, "Do you mean to say they could be rounding Diamond Head and you wouldn't know it?" The officer lamely responded, "I hope they would have been spotted before now."

At that moment, the Japanese fleet was approaching the staging area—Latitude 42 N, Longitude 170 W—to await the final attack orders. *Akagi* pilot Zenji Abe said, "It was not yet decided to commence hostilities at the time, merely to deploy for war." The final signal to attack waited for the emperor's approval. At midmorning on December 3, Yamamoto was summoned to the palace to receive the Imperial Rescript. "I, the Emperor, on the occasion of ordering the expedition, leave the matter up to you, as the Commander in Chief of the Combined Fleet." Yamamoto responded, "I am overwhelmed to receive, prior to the declaration of war, such a generous Imperial Rescript." The die was cast; First Air Fleet sailed eastward into the "vacant sea," an area of the ocean between the main shipping route from Hawaii to Japan and China and the northern great circle route near the

Above: Flight deck of *Akagi* on the way to Pearl Harbor. Note two other carriers just visible at top center. *History Division, USMC*

Opposite: Aboard the *Akagi* as it proceeds along the northern route to Pearl Harbor. Note heavy cold weather clothing and that the machine guns are manned and ready. *History Division, USMC*

Aleutians. It was almost devoid of ships, the perfect route to launch a surprise attack.

There was a downside to the northern route, however. It was subject to extended periods of bad weather, which played havoc with refueling. Only seven ships could make it all the way to Pearl Harbor without taking on fuel. Every ship crammed extra barrels of fuel into every nook and cranny, which required special approval at the NGS level. However, even with this unusual approach, Nagumo's destroyers had to be refueled every day. Lieutenant Commander Sadao Chigusa, executive officer of the destroyer *Akigumo*, wrote in his diary, "We refueled astern very slowly. The towing line broke. Very dangerous . . . we tried again to refuel but it became dark and we gave up." Not only was it a dangerous procedure— several sailors were swept overboard—but it slowed the

Japanese carriers sailing toward Pearl Harbor. *History Division, USMC*

fleet from its normal twelve to fourteen knots to nine knots. Despite the hardships, Nagumo's force reached the staging area on schedule.

During the late afternoon of December 2, Nagumo was in his sea cabin with the chief of staff. Their conversation was interrupted by an officer bearing a flimsy naval message form. The admiral took it and quickly scanned the communiqué: "*Niitaka Yama Nobore* [Climb Mt. Niitaka]." Nagumo was visibly moved—it was Yamamoto's signal to attack. He handed it to his chief of staff, Rear Admiral Ryunosuke Kusaka, who later wrote, "When we were given this [message], we felt the apprehension that had made us worry so long suddenly disappear. I felt then that my mind was as clear as the autumn

moon in the sky." Nagumo penned a proclamation, which was read to all the sailors of the fleet: "A gigantic fleet is concentrated at Pearl Harbor. This fleet must be destroyed . . . for this, the Imperial Navy has concentrated the cream of its forces in order to ensure success. Heaven is witness to the justice of our cause." His words unleashed a frenzy of patriotic enthusiasm. The crews erupted over and over again with the traditional "*Banzai*," literally, "ten thousand years," originally an expression for wishing the emperor a long life. Four days later, the fleet refueled for the last time. The tankers split off and headed for the rendezvous point. The crews lined the rails and waved their caps in salute to the attack force. The fleet went to battle speed, twenty-four knots.

Opposite: Antiaircraft crews of the Japanese carrier *Akagi. History Division, USMC*

Japanese "Val" dive-bomber photographed just as its bomb was released, probably during the first minutes of the attack.
National Archives 80-G-32460

CHAPTER FOUR

SUNDAY MORNING INFAMY

"General Quarters, No Shit, Japanese Bombers!"

—Captain Chevey S. White, USMC
Officer of the Deck, USS *Tennessee*

Lieutenant Colonel Pfeiffer of Kimmel's staff was deeply worried. "In the early days of December, there had been enough Washington messages to cover any possible contingency; that is, no matter what happened in the future, someone could point to a message that should have covered the situation. For instance, we received a message saying, 'Go on alert, but do not alarm the people.' That directed an impossibility. Hawaii is so self-contained and the military and navy were so much a part of the community that everybody on the island would know if the troops and naval personnel were standing by on alert. Many messages on the 6th all pointed to Japan making its main effort for a war in Malaya."

0530, December 7: First Air Fleet reaches a point six hundred miles north and slightly west of Oahu. The fleet is on high alert because it is within range of American B-17 Martin bombers, but too far away to launch their own aircraft. Six hours later, at precisely 1130, Nagumo's force turned due south for the final sprint to the launch point.

The flagship broke out the historic "Z" pennant that Admiral Togo had hoisted at Tsushima in his victory over the Russian fleet.

Pfeiffer was planning on working a half day on December 6. "During the noon hour Admiral Kimmel came into the Plans office where Captain McMorris and I were preparing to leave. Admiral Kimmel said his stomach was acting up, because he felt he did not know the whole story and frankly was worried. I believe he had a keener awareness of the situation than any of his staff. Captain McMorris tried to console him by making light of the situation, but Admiral Kimmel was not impressed, nor mentally relieved."

Captain Jack Earle tried not to be critical as *Arizona* made fast to Fox 7, her mooring quay on battleship row. His ship, USS *Tennessee*, was next in line, alongside the USS *West Virginia*, which gave him an excellent vantage point to observe his new command. Earle was in receipt of orders directing him to "report to Commanding Officer USS *Arizona* BB-39, as commanding officer of the

Brigadier General Omar T. Pfeiffer, USMC, after the war. He holds a Japanese slogan board that he found in an enemy dugout on Peleliu. *US Marine Corps*

his way to his new command. "Major Shapley met me on the quarterdeck late in the day and formally presented me to the ship's captain, Captain Van Valkenburgh, as his relief." Shapley was anxious to complete the change of command. "I had just made major had received orders back to Camp Elliott in California and leave with my family before reporting to the 2nd Marine Division." However, before the official change of command could occur, the two had to complete the time-honored inventory of the detachment's clothing and property: "jocks, socks, and sundries."

Private Leo DeVere Amundson also reported aboard about the same time. Private First Class Lamar Crawford met him at the gangway. "I arranged for his assignment to a bunk space. Further assignment to a squad, duty section, and a battle station were deferred, pending interviews with the new Detachment Commander and the First Sergeant." Crawford said that no one in the detachment was given liberty because they were standing by to meet the new commanding officer. He was not bothered, however. "I didn't go out too much. I didn't drink like some of the other Marines—and beside, there wasn't much to do."

Earle did not have time to pay his respects to Lieutenant Colonel Daniel "Danny" R. Fox, the senior Marine on board. Fox was the battleship division Marine officer and served on the staff of Rear Admiral Kidd. Although Fox was not in the detachment chain of command, protocol demanded that Earle introduce himself "at the earliest convenient time." Danny Fox, although recently promoted (June 1941), was an old-timer, having served as an enlisted Marine in World War I. As a sergeant in the 17th Company, 5th Marines, he distinguished himself in combat and was awarded the Navy Cross, the Army Distinguished Service Cross, the Purple Heart, and the French Croix de Guerre. The Navy Cross citation noted:

"For Extraordinary heroism in action near St. Etienne on October 4, 1918. He volunteered and carried an important message across a heavily shelled area, returning through a barrage to report the results of his mission. Later, after being wounded, he remained on duty for four hours, carrying messages across a field swept by machine-gun fire."

Fox was discharged at the end of the war and returned home to Pottstown, Pennsylvania. A year and a half later he applied for a commission and was accepted in the Student Officers' School at Philadelphia. He successfully completed the course and received a commission in

Marine detachment." Although he was happy to get the command, he was disappointed to leave "the best ship in the fleet." He was being promoted out of the job. "My promotion to captain in the fall of 1941 made me over-rank for the *Tennessee* Marine detachment, which was already commanded by a captain." His friend, Captain Chevey White, had the assignment.

Earle had received the orders weeks earlier but had not been able to carry them out because of the fleet's operational schedule. "The reason for the delay was that the *Tennessee* was flagship of BATDIV 2, while the *Arizona* was the flag in BATDIV 1, and for several weeks the Pacific Battle Fleet had rotated in and out of Pearl Harbor in divided groupings, with BATDIVS 2 and 4 at sea while the odd-numbered BATDIVS were tied up in Pearl Harbor, with crews on liberty." December 6 was the first time in weeks that the battleships were all in port at the same time. Earle gathered his gear and made

1921. Fox went on to serve in overseas and stateside assignments. As a major, he was selected to attend the Army Infantry School. It marked him as an officer with a bright future. He was hand-selected for his current assignment on the admiral's staff.

Immediately after talking with Captain Van Valkenburgh, the two officers commenced taking the inventory. At 2100, they found themselves in the bowels of the ship, "hot as hell," working up a powerful thirst. "Jack," Shapley suggested, "let's go ashore and get a beer." Earle did not need a second invitation. They caught a boat to the landing and walked from there to the officer's club. It was filled with junior officers, couples, and geographical bachelors (married officers whose wives were stateside), all in formal attire—the "O" club's regulations did not allow informal wear after 1700. Shapley was a geographical bachelor. The Earles, on the other hand, lived in a "termite-infested cheap wooden apartment building on the corner of Aloha Drive and Seaside Avenue in Waikiki." The rent was sixty dollars a month, a big hit for a junior officer. To supplement their income, Barbara Earle worked for Naval Intelligence, which occupied an office in the Young Hotel on Bishop Street.

Shapley spotted a group of *Arizona* officers celebrating a birthday and joined the party. Earle was introduced and enjoyed a drink with the relaxed crowd. At one point, Shapley turned to him and suggested, "Why don't you go home to your wife and come back in the morning to finish the inventory."

"Because Alan Shapley wanted a beer, I'm alive today," Earle related, somewhat tongue in cheek. Earle settled up and caught a cab—Charley's Taxis, the only company authorized to come on base—for the twenty-minute drive home. There was little traffic going into the city. His taxi was able to make good time at that hour and arrived home a little after 10:00 p.m. However, the other lane was crowded with buses and taxis rushing sailors and Marines back to the base before liberty expired at midnight (Cinderella liberty). The bars, tattoo parlors, and whorehouses on Hotel Street emptied quickly as the men scrambled to find transportation. The Shore Patrol cleared the area, sweeping up those men too drunk to make it back on their own and took them back to their ship, "for their own good." They also broke up the occasional fight but, for the most part, it was a typical Saturday night on Oahu.

2400, December 7: First Air Fleet reaches a point approximately four hundred miles north of Oahu without being discovered. Air Officer Genda is on the bridge of the flagship Akagi. *"I was absolutely sure of the success of the air raid."*

0030: Japanese aircraft mechanics begin last-minute checks of the strike aircraft. The attack pilots eat an early breakfast of plums and rice. Many wear white clothes marked "Sure Victory" under their flight helmets.

Private First Class James E. Cory stood the 2400 to 0200 gangway watch with the officer of the deck. He was mildly amused watching three inebriated sailors negotiate the steep ladder to the quarterdeck, until one vomited on the deck. It wasn't funny anymore, someone had to clean it up—and the smell would "gag a maggot." Just as the OD looked his way, a petty officer handed the miscreant a bucket and a mop. "Clean up your own puke, sailor," he growled. The drunk's two buddies just barely managed to keep from laughing at his misfortune, but the look on the petty officer's face spelled trouble if they dared move a muscle. Cory remembered later that "for the most part, the returning seamen were clean and sober, only a few were under the weather. You see more rowdiness at a high school football game than you'd see in a whole fleet liberty in Honolulu. . . ." At the end of his watch, Cory turned in and was sound asleep in minutes, secure in the knowledge that he could sleep in; Sunday was his day off.

0100: The large long-range Japanese submarine I-16 released its midget submarine seven miles off the entrance to Pearl Harbor. Fifteen minutes later I-22 released a second, followed by I-18, 1-20, and I-24. The last midget sub was released at 0333. The attack had begun.

The fire watch stumbled through the darkened Marine compartment until he found the right hammock. He gently shook the sleeping figure until the man grunted that he was awake. Corporal Michael Soley swung out of the hammock and made his way to the head, where he performed his morning ablutions. He quickly donned his uniform and made his way through the passageways to the main deck, where it was still dark. The sky was just starting to lighten. He could see well enough to make his way across the teak deck without stumbling over the tie-downs. Several other watchstanders passed him on the way to their Condition III stations (two 5-inch antiaircraft guns manned and ready, one on each side of the ship). Soley reached the mainmast tripod and began to climb swiftly to his station in secondary aft. Countless ascents had inured him to the dizzying height. He was not even breathing hard as he

Japanese "Val" dive-bomber taking off for Pearl Harbor. Note crewmen cheering him on. *History Division, USMC*

climbed through the cupola's hatch. He put on the sound-powered headset—a communications system that didn't require an external power source—and settled down for another boring four-hour watch.

0530: The Japanese heavy cruisers Tone *and* Chikuma *launched two Type O Aichi E 13A1 "Jake" floatplanes for a reconnaissance of Pearl Harbor and the Pacific Fleet's alternate anchorage at Lahaina.*

Private First Class Lamar Crawford got up at reveille—0600. "I had breakfast in the Marine's main deck living and sleeping quarters. After breakfast, I checked my locker's contents—shoes and clothing—thinking that I would get ready for Protestant Church service which were scheduled for 0900. In the meantime, I checked out and cleaned my assigned firearm, a 1903 Springfield rifle."

Private First Class George Richmond Bailey hurried through the passageway. He was running a little late and didn't want to hold up his buddy, Private Russell J. McCurdy. He reached flag country and spotted McCurdy standing at ease outside Admiral Kidd's stateroom. The two exchanged good-natured pleasantries and then McCurdy passed on what he knew of the admiral's schedule for the morning. At that, he took off, leaving Bailey standing in his spot. McCurdy went directly to his compartment, shucked off his soiled uniform, and went to the head to clean up. A civilian family had invited him, and others of the crew, to spend the day and have dinner with them.

0615: The Japanese aircraft carriers turn into the wind and prepare to launch the first strike, 183 aircraft—43 fighters, 49 high-level bombers, 51 dive bombers, and 40

Flight deck of the Japanese carrier *Akagi*. Note splinter shields protecting the bridge area. *History Division, USMC*

torpedo planes. The carriers pitch and roll in the heavy swells. The first aircraft speeds down the flight deck, lurches into the air, but drops precipitously toward the dark water. The deck crew holds their breath as the bomb-laden aircraft struggles to gain altitude. They heave a sigh of relief as it rises and heads for the rendezvous point. Twenty minutes later, the flight decks are clear. The first wave is safely launched.

0637: USS Ward *sights a "suspicious object," goes to general quarters, and attacks.*

0651: USS Ward *reports, "We have dropped depth charges upon sub operating in defensive area."*

Lieutenant Simensen was up early. He had duty as the junior officer of the deck, and he wanted to make sure his white uniform was squared away. A last-minute dubbing on his white shoes, run an iron over his blouse and trousers, and he would be ready to go. He was a little envious of his roommate, First Lieutenant John P.

Coursey, who had the day off and was probably enjoying himself at the beach. Maybe next weekend the tables would be turned.

0715: The second strike is launched, 168 aircraft—36 fighters, 54 horizontal bombers, and 78 dive bombers. Squadron Leader Lieutenant Zenji Abe noted that "the ship was rolling and pitching, but not enough for me to worry. I felt as if it were just another routine exercise."

First Sergeant Duveene and Gunny Holzworth, as was their habit, rose early to check the duty log to see if anything unusual had happened during the night. Satisfied that all was well in the world, they headed for the chief's lounge for breakfast. Major Shapley had also decided on an early breakfast. "I was going to play baseball with the

Japanese "Val" dive-bomber pulling off its attack.
National Archives 80-G-32671

baseball team. I was the coach and first baseman. We'd won the Battle Force championship and were scheduled to play the team from the USS *Enterprise*, which, unknown to me, had been delayed at sea."

0740: Commander Fuchida sights the coastline of Oahu's Kahuku Point through the clouds and signals the first wave to take up attack formations. The formation opens fanwise—the dive bombers climbed to 14,375 feet, the torpedo planes descended to sea level, and the high-altitude bombers took station at 9,845 feet.

0753: The first strike attacks. Fuchida orders his radioman to send the code words, "Tora, Tora, Tora" (Tiger, Tiger, Tiger), meaning they have achieved surprise. Aboard the Nagato, *Yamamoto is handed Fuchida's signal.*

Corporal Soley, high in the mainmast, watched the

Above: Japanese "Val" headed for its target. *National Archives 80-G-32629*

Left: The USS *California*, victim to two torpedo hits and one bomb, sinks into the harbor. *History Division, USMC*

Nevada's band and color guard. He was impressed with the scene—white uniforms of the sailors—blue Marine blouses—perfectly aligned formation. Suddenly, his attention was drawn to a diving aircraft. "What the hell," he exclaimed, as it roared overhead. It was so close he could see red circles on the wings and fuselage. He heard the unmistakable sound of a machine gun and *Nevada*'s formation scattered like a covey of quail. It suddenly dawned on him what he was seeing, and he shouted into his sound-powered headset, "Jap planes!"

0755–0825: The first strike force, twenty-four Japanese torpedo planes and twenty-seven dive bombers, attacks the ships moored on the west and northwest of Ford Island.

Lieutenant Goto was "shocked to see the row of battleships in front of my eyes . . . I flew diagonally not knowing which was the bow and which was the stern. All I saw was the mast, the bridge, and smokestack. I said 'Fire.' The plane lightened, as the torpedo was released. I saw two water columns go up and smoothly go down."

Above: Japanese "Val" dive-bomber pulling off the target. *National Archives 80-G-32644*

Right: A torpedo passed under the minelayer USS *Oglala*, which had been the outboard ship, and struck the USS *Helena*'s forward engine room, killing thirty-three sailors. The *Oglala*, also damaged, was moved to avoid pinning the light cruiser *Helena* to the dock. The *Oglala* capsized after two hours of taking on water. *US Navy*

Crawford "stepped outside the Marine compartment onto the port-side quarterdeck. As I came into the bright light I heard the sound of airplane engines, several of them. Looking up, I saw a Japanese dive bomber coming directly toward the *Arizona*. About that time, machine-gun bullets from the plane started bouncing off the tub-type gun mount immediately to my right. I realized immediately that we were being attacked. The machine-gun bullets were bouncing all over and seemed to be addressed to 'whom it may concern.' I did a quick dash into the Marine compartment."

Lieutenant Simensen ran to the admiral's gangway to see what was causing the large column of smoke over Ford Island. The OOD joined him. Suddenly stray bullets hit the teak deck, sending fragments and splinters flying around them. The OOD yelled to the boatswain mate of the watch to sound the air raid alarm—three blasts of a warning howler over the 1MC, the shipboard public address system—and grabbed a phone to notify Captain Van Valkenburgh. Lieutenant Simensen ran to his air raid station, as the captain came on deck. Private Don E. Hamel, the duty field music, sounded the air defense call, a strident series of short notes that were guaranteed to get everyone's attention.

Captain Chevey White was on the quarterdeck of the USS *Tennessee* as the first Japanese planes swept down. He immediately reacted. "Sound general quarters," he shouted. The Marine field music flipped the switch of

Above: Japanese "Val" starting its run. *History Division, USMC*

Right: Japanese attacker pulling off the target. *National Archives 80-G-32436*

the 1MC and sounded the call. The crew thought it was a drill and did not respond quickly enough to satisfy the thoroughly keyed-up Marine. Exasperated, he shouted into the microphone, "General quarters, no shit, Japanese bombers!" (Captain White was killed in action at the head of his battalion on Guam, July 22, 1944.)

Corporal Earl Nightingale did not have an antiaircraft station. "I ran to the port hatch leading to the quarterdeck and saw a bomb strike a barge of some sort alongside the *Nevada*, or in that vicinity. I could distinctly hear machine-gun fire. At this point our antiaircraft battery opened up." Private Russell McCurdy was on deck. "I saw men pointing upwards, some with faces white and scared, others looking out portholes. I saw bombs hitting Ford Island and they knocked down the water tower."

Major Shapley ran out on the fantail. "The crew was lined up along the rail looking toward the Pearl Harbor shipyard. A lot of planes were coming in from Pearl Harbor. I saw a destroyer on the marine railway demolished and another destroyer in drydock, the USS *Pennsylvania*, and another destroyer burst into flames. Debris was flying all over the place. I saw splinters flying up on deck and I realized we were being strafed." Corporal Soley had a grandstand seat. From his position in the mainmast, he could see almost the entire anchorage—battleship row, Ford Island, submarine pens, and hospital point—all the major facilities in the harbor. He was almost overcome with a flood of emotion as he watched ship after ship take bomb and torpedo hits—geysers

The forward magazine of the USS *Shaw* explodes during the Japanese attack. She suffered three bomb hits. *US Navy 16871*

erupted mainmast high, smoke and flames billowed from badly damaged ships. Ford Island seemed to be on fire, as hangar after hangar burned to their steel framework. The noise was terrific, explosions, gunfire, ship alarms—it was mind numbing.

Captain Earle was asleep when he heard someone shouting and banging on his apartment door. He jumped out of bed, hurried to the door, and found his neighbor—Commander John McKillip, a naval officer on the Commander in Chief Pacific (CincPac) Staff—shouting, "Pearl Harbor is under attack!" He rushed to the lanai, where he saw the black puffs of antiaircraft fire over the harbor. He quickly donned civilian clothes—Barbara Earle claimed

Above: A view of Ford Island from a Japanese plane just as the *West Virginia*, on the far side of the island, takes a torpedo hit. Two other Japanese planes are visible, one over Ford Island and another over the Navy Yard at far right.

Opposite top: A seaplane hanger in flames at the Pearl Harbor Naval Air Station on the southern tip of Ford Island. *History Division, USMC*

Opposite bottom: The burned-out remains of the seaplane hanger. *History Division, USMC*

Damage from the attack was not limited to the military installations. Civilian areas took hits as well, as shown by these bullet-riddled cars. *Honolulu Star-Bulletin*

he was out the door in five minutes. Earle remembered, "Lieutenant John Alford, a friend from the *Tennessee*, and I flagged down a taxi and raced for Pearl Harbor."

Lieutenant Colonel Pfeiffer did not have any duty, so he slept late. "About 0800 I was awakened by people talking loudly outside my room. I arose, went out to see what the occasion was, and shortly thereafter my telephone rang. It was the flag secretary telling me of the Japanese attack and to report immediately to Pearl Harbor. I dressed quickly and in minutes was on the road. There was some strafing along the road but none came near to me. Jap dive bombing was still in progress when I arrived at headquarters about 0830."

Private First Class Cory was on the second armored deck. "As I was coming back past Turret No. 2, some very husky sailor came down this ladder and shouted, 'Japs! We're being attacked by Japs!' There were people sitting around coffee pots in their skivvy shirts waiting for the coffee to brew. They looked up at him, and somebody started to say something in a kidding voice, but right behind him came another man saying, 'Jap planes! Jap planes! We're being bombed!' Well, these guys were really moving. I don't think anybody in the compartment took more than a second or two to be convinced that this was an attack. Then right on the tail of this came the air-raid siren. Also over the loudspeaker came the air-defense call blown by the field music of the day."

Bailey felt the ship vibrate, but did not know why. Suddenly, Admiral Kidd threw open the door and rushed out, still buttoning his blouse. Bailey followed as the

admiral hurried toward the signal bridge. They passed several gun crews going into action. Kidd shouted words of encouragement. Lieutenant Colonel Fox and the rest of the admiral's staff quickly joined him on the signal bridge. At the same time, Captain Van Valkenburgh made his way to the navigation bridge and assumed command of the ship.

Cory rushed topside to casemate nine. "In this casemate was a 'bay window,' which gave me a view out over Ford Island and the *Tennessee*. Some sailor said, 'Look, there's a Jap plane.' It looked much like a Spitfire, except that the wheels were fixed types. It just cleared the after-deck of the *Tennessee*. We saw a plane over Ford Island start smoking, and then we felt the impact of bullets on the casemate overhead. A plane dived over Ford Island heading toward us. It was a dive bomber. It released something from beneath it. I recognized that it was a bomb, but I was fascinated by the sight of it because this was the first bomb I'd seen in war headed in my general direction. It looked like it was oblong when it left the airplane, but then it began to get like a basketball, then briefly it turned oblong again and flashed into the sea between the stern of the *Tennessee* and the dredge pipeline." Then sailors came running back from the hatch. They were white; they were scared! I began to get frightened also. I don't know about other people, but I thought, 'Gee, I might get killed!'"

The word was passed for "all unengaged personnel to get below the third deck," which was armored and would furnish more protection. Cory remembered, "A navy officer

Wreckage of a Japanese "Zero" brought down at Pearl Harbor. *National Archives 80-G-73040*

Secretary of the Navy Commendation Second Lieutenant Carleton E. Simensen

"Second Lieutenant Carleton Elliott Simensen. For heroic leadership and devotion to duty during the attack on the U.S. Pacific Fleet in Pearl Harbor, T. H., by Japanese forces on December 7, 1941. During the first few moments of the attack on the USS *Arizona*, he led the Marines up the exposed ladders of the mainmast in spite of the heavy bombing and strafing attack. Upon reaching the searchlight platform he was mortally wounded. He died almost instantly but not before he mentioned to the Marine personnel not to assist him but to continue to their battle stations in secondary aft. His courage and gallant leadership are an inspiration to all."

came through the compartment, waving his hands and saying, 'Everybody below the armored deck! Get below!' I went down the hatch, but just as I put my foot on the ladder to go below, general quarters sounded."

Major Shapley knew why. "The *Pennsylvania*, flagship of the whole fleet, put up the signal, 'Go to general quarters.' There was a little bit of confusion, people started going down the ladders and now people were going the other way too." Lieutenant Simensen pushed his way into the crowd and restored order, clearing the way to the ladder. Shapley commended his action, "Lieutenant Simensen did quite a job of turning the sailors around, so we could get out of the compartment." The two officers rushed for their GQ station in secondary aft.

As the order "All hands man your battle stations!" blared from the speakers, Corporal Bond raced to his gun in number ten casemate. He took the ladder in three gigantic leaps and reached the compartment in record time. His crew piled in right behind him. He quickly held a muster and ordered them to their action stations. Despite the fact that his broadside gun could not be used against aircraft, Bond did as he was trained to do—prepare for action. Sergeant John M. Baker and Corporal Earl C. Nightingale passed through the casemate. "The gun was already manned and we heard Corporal Bond yell, 'Train out ninety.' The men seemed extremely calm and collected." One by one, the gun captains reported that they were manned and ready to First Sergeant Duveene and Gunny Holzworth, as they calmly walked through the casemates. Duveene spotted Henry Kalinowski and gave him the usual, "Go Champion!"

0805: A five-hundred-pound bomb glances off the number four turret, penetrates the deck, and explodes in the flag officer's pantry.

Cory rushed to his post in secondary aft. "I started up this inclined leg on the starboard side. When I got about two-thirds up, there was a slap aft—a very heavy slap—and then you felt the deck of the *Arizona* being penetrated, and then you heard the bomb explosion. A bomb hit aft on the slanting part of Turret No. 4. I saw this when I looked down later. There was a bomb splash, as we called it, because the bomb had hit the slanting side of the turret and glanced off it and exploded in officers' country. It literally wiped out most of the officers aboard the *Arizona*." Ensign G. S. Flannigan was in the lower handling room of Turret No. 3. "When the bomb hit, it made a whish with a gust of hot air and sparks flew. The lights went out and a very nauseating gas and smoke filled the compartment."

Crawford "found Amundson sitting on a bench just inside the Marines' area. He was very frightened and confused. I stopped and talked with him until general quarters sounded. I told him to 'sit down right there, and stay until this is over.' I crossed through the compartment to the starboard side, up the ladder to the boat deck, then mounted the tripod ladder for the eighty-foot exposed climb to my battle station in the secondary control booth." Amundson would be listed as killed in action.

Lieutenant Simensen led a file of men up the starboard mainmast ladder. They were totally exposed. Bullets and shrapnel filled the air, making snapping sounds as the lethal metal hurtled through the air. Corporal Nightingale "could hear fragments whistling past."

Sergeant Baker was close behind Simensen. "Just as the lieutenant reached the first platform of the mainmast and stepped clear of the superstructure, a bomb hit somewhere on the quarterdeck." A piece of shrapnel tore into Simensen's midsection. He fell back against Shapley, almost knocking him off the ladder. "Simensen fell back into my arms. I boosted him up to the searchlight platform." The lieutenant was obviously dying; tremendous blood loss, skin pale, eyelids fluttering. Nothing could be

Smoke billows from the shattered Arizona. West Virginia and Tennessee are in the background. *National Archives 80-G-32689*

done, so Shapley continued to his post. Corporal Nightingale reached the same conclusion. "I saw Second Lieutenant Simensen laying on his back with blood on his shirt front. I bent over him and, taking him by the shoulders, asked if there was anything I could do. He was dead, or nearly, so that speech was impossible. Seeing there was nothing I could do, I continued to my battle station."

Cory said, "I ran up the ladder just as fast as I could and came to rest against Lamar Crawford's back, because he was blocking my way. I started to step around him and I saw the reason for his delay. There was Lieutenant Simensen, one of the most popular officers on the *Arizona*, lying in a pool of blood. I said, 'Oh, my God! This is for real!' His whole abdomen and lower chest were just

Japanese planes fly through antiaircraft fire over Pearl Harbor. *History Division, USMC*

Residents inspect a damaged home in Honolulu. The damage was probably caused by an American antiaircraft shell falling back to the ground. *Honolulu Star-Bulletin*

Residents assist fire fighters. These small fires were most likely started by improperly fused American antiaircraft shells falling into residential areas, not Japanese attacks. *Honolulu Star-Bulletin*

torn to bits—probably by splinters. He was losing blood in such volume that he couldn't last much longer. Too weak to talk, he moved his lips to form the words, 'Leave me. Go on!'"

Upon entering secondary aft, Shapley found Corporal Soley none the worse for wear, even though the cupola was completely exposed. In quick succession, Nightingale, Baker, Cory, Crawford, McCurdy, Privates First Class Edward James Braham, Frank Robert Cabiness, Kenneth D. Goodman, and Donald G. Young, and Private Lawrence Hardy reported. All had remarkably close calls and were pretty shaken up. Cory probably spoke for all when he described his own feelings: "By this time I was literally scared out of my wits. There were bullets ringing into secondary aft, and you could feel the impact of them on the metal as you went up the various ladders and into secondary aft." Nightingale reported and noticed "a lot of talking going on"—a normal reaction to stress—"and I shouted for silence, which came immediately"—ingrained discipline. Shapley was frustrated because "communications at this time had gone out, and we were unable to do anything. I controlled ten guns of the secondary battery, which was not an antiaircraft battery. We couldn't elevate the guns high enough to do any damage to the planes. Indeed should I have been firing, I'd have shot Ford Island on one side or Pearl Harbor on the other."

Crawford remembered "sailors manning the 'bird bath' [a .50-caliber station above the mainmast] quickly expending their two hundred rounds of ready ammunition. They climbed into secondary aft saying, 'Do you mind if we join you?'"

Private McCurdy stared with utter fascination at the scene outside the glass windows of the cupola. "I observed torpedo planes in the attack and the pullout. The planes seemed only an arm length away. So close, and the pullout speed was so slow you could read their faces as they slid their canopies. I saw the USS *Oklahoma* roll over like a wounded whale."

The line of battleships responded to the attack. Nightingale saw that *Arizona*'s "antiaircraft guns were in full action, firing very rapidly." Black puffballs filled the sky over Pearl Harbor, as the 5-inch antiaircraft shells exploded. Unfortunately, many of their fuses were not set at the proper altitude and fell on Honolulu and the surrounding area, causing several civilian deaths and quite a bit of property damage.

Captain Earle remembered a Hawaiian woman who sold flowers on the weekend. "She always sang out, 'Flowers, flowers, flowers.' Suddenly there was a large explosion—an improperly fused five-inch antiaircraft shell landed in the area. The woman paused for a long moment and then resumed her chant, as if nothing had happened!"

One leg of the tripod has been severed, causing *Arizona*'s charred foremast to tilt forward over the remains of the bridge.
National Archives 80-G-32420

CHAPTER FIVE

FIRE ON THE WATER

"A hateful, mean-looking red flame."
—Commander Mitsuo Fuchida
Leader, Pearl Harbor Strike Force

0812–1813: A high-level bomber group, composed of five planes, flying in a "V" formation attacked the Arizona *and the repair ship USS* Vestal, *moored alongside. Lieutenant Shojira Kondo, at a height of 10,480 feet, released his armor-piercing bomb, which struck the starboard side of the forecastle deck, near Turret No. 2. It penetrated four decks before exploding.*

Private First Class Richard Fiske, Field Music USS *West Virginia*, "remembered the shock of watching the path of a slow-moving bomb. At first I thought it would hit the *West Virginia*, then watching it draw closer, change direction, and fall into the *Arizona*. I saw the ship transformed into a ball of fire, and men thrown high into the air. The shock wave threw me back against the bridge, and the captain, standing next to me was mortally wounded by shrapnel."

High above, Lieutenant Commander Fuchida saw a terrific explosion. "The flame and smoke erupted skyward together," he recalled. "It was a hateful, mean-looking red flame, the kind that powder produces, and I knew at once that a big magazine had exploded. My plane shuddered in the suction of the after-blast."

Cory described the hit. "The bomb struck forward of us. You could feel it penetrate the decks, and then there was this big 'Whoosh!' Now it wasn't a Bang. It wasn't a Boom. It was Whoosh! My watch stopped between 0812 and 0813." McCurdy remembered, "The terrible explo-

sion caused the ship to toss and shake violently. The ship was shaking, tossing, and went up out of the water, and then the bow rose up forty feet into the air and opened up like the petal of a flower. The mainmast quivered and turned our control station into a dice box. We were shaken into a human ball." Seaman Second Class Oree C. Weller was thrown to the deck. "The mainmast vibrated as though undergoing an earthquake. Flames burst through the smoke as the ammunition in the magazines continued to explode and fuel oil from the ruptured tanks ignited. The noise of the ammunition explosions and the fuel fires was deafening." Nightingale thought that "everything seemed aflame forward of the mainmast."

A searing blast of flame tore through the ship. Hundreds of men were killed or severely burned in an instant. The Marine gun crews in the casemates were cut down where they stood. Those that survived were more dead than alive. Cory was horrified at what he saw. "These people were zombies, in essence. They were burned completely white. Their skin was just as white as if you'd taken a bucket of whitewash and painted it white. Their hair was burned off; their eyebrows were burned off; the pitiful remains of their uniforms in their crotch was a charred remnant; and the insoles of their shoes were about the only thing that was left on these bodies. They were moving like robots, and they were

Smoke obscures *Arizona*'s bow. *National Archives 80-G-72410*

stumbling along the decks. These were burned men!" Corporal Bond, the only man to make it out of number ten casemate, was one of those "walking dead."

The men in the mainmast were lucky because, as Cory explained, "the bridge shielded us from the flames coming aft. There was at least eight hundred feet of very massive structure that shielded us from this." But there was still mortal danger. McCurdy remembered, "Parts of the ship, flames, and bomb fragments flew by reaching hundreds of feet into the air. The ship's midsection opened like a blooming flower, burning white hot within. Our entire magazine and forward oil storage had exploded; tons of TNT and thousands of gallons of fuel oil poured into the water. Black smoke billowed into the sky as the oil caught fire." Cory spoke about his reaction. "We cringed there. You have an instant, automatic response. I think that at

this moment I wanted to flee, but this was impossible. You're on station, you're in combat; you can't leave until you're given permission, and nobody's going to ask permission to leave."

Ensign D. Hein was in the navigation bridge with Captain Van Valkenburgh and the quartermaster. "Suddenly the whole bridge shook like it was an earthquake; flame came through the bridge windows, which had been broken by gunfire. We three were trying to get out the port door at the aft end of the bridge during all this shaking,

Arizona as seen from Ford Island. Mainmast battle station where Major Shapley and his Marines were stationed is in the center of the photo. *National Archives 80-G-32041*

but could not. We staggered to the starboard side and fell on the deck just forward of the wheel. I raised my head and saw the port door was open and I got up and ran through it." Hein was able to escape, but Captain Van

Destroyed forward section of *Arizona*. Note the .50-caliber machine guns in the "birdbath" atop the unscathed mainmast at upper right. *National Archives 80-G-32427*

Valkenburgh and the quartermaster succumbed to the flames. Admiral Kidd, his staff, Lieutenant Colonel Fox, and Bailey died on the signal bridge. Salvage crews searching through the smoldering wreckage three days later found what was believed to be Admiral Kidd's body on the boat deck, at the foot of the bridge ladder. They also found Van Valkenburgh's academy ring in a pile of ash.

A Japanese 1,756-pound armor-piercing bomb touched off 582 tons of 14-inch ordnance in the forward magazine. The resulting conflagration caused a massive explosion that swept through the ship, killing 1,177 members of her crew.

Shapley soon realized that the situation was impossible. "We watched the ship list, which was rather terrifying. I thought we were all going to get cooked to death because I couldn't see anything but fire below. However, after about twenty minutes or more, one of the tripod legs became clear of flames, and I saw the opportunity to get to the main deck. 'We'd better go below,' I shouted. 'We're no good here.'" Crawford remembered Shapley saying, "Well, men, this is it. Abandon ship. It's every

Arizona's mainmast stands outlined against the clouds; the foremast has disappeared within the oily smoke rising from her decks. *History Division, USMC*

man for himself. Good luck and God bless you all!" McCurdy said that Shapley's calmness and skilled leadership gave him the courage to remain calm and alert.

Sergeant Baker was the first to start down the ladder, followed by McCurdy and Soley. "We proceeded down the ladder on the portside tripod leg. The heat was oven temperature, and the flames licked close by at times. Fortunately, we were protected by a slight breeze from the port quarter. The rails on the ladder were hot, causing slight burns to our hands." Cory was the sixth man through the hatch. "I was right beside it, and I wanted to be the first one out, but I forced myself to wait until some other men had gone first. I was confused along with being scared, but not so confused that I wanted to run." Nightingale followed Shapley. "I was the last man to leave secondary aft because I looked around and there was no one left. I followed the major down the port side of the tripod mast."

Baker reached the searchlight platform. "Someone hollered, 'You can't use the ladder.' PFC Hardy jumped and landed on Turret No. 3." Crawford saw him jump.

Medal of Honor Citation
Rear Admiral Isaac C. Kidd, USN

"For conspicuous devotion to duty, extraordinary courage, and complete disregard of his own life, during the attack on the Fleet in Pearl Harbor, Territory of Hawaii, by Japanese Forces on December 7, 1941. He immediately went to the bridge and as Commander Battleship Division One, courageously discharged his duties as Senior Officer Present Afloat until the USS *Arizona*, his Flagship, blew up from magazine explosions and a direct bomb hit on the bridge, which resulted in the loss of his life."

Painting of Admiral Kidd as a Rear Admiral, portrait by Robert Rishell. *Naval Historical Center NH 85226-KN*

Medal of Honor Endorsement
Lieutenant Colonel Daniel R. Fox

Lieutenant Colonel Daniel R. Fox was recommended for the Medal of Honor by Colonel Harry K. Pickett, the commanding officer of the Marine Forces of the Fourteenth Naval District. The recommendation was endorsed by the Commandant, Lieutenant General Thomas Holcomb. The endorsement stated: "It is recommended that the Medal of Honor be posthumously awarded the late Lieutenant Colonel Daniel R. Fox, USMC, who was killed on the Flag Bridge or on his way to the Flag Bridge which was his battle station aboard the USS *Arizona* on the morning of the attack on Pearl Harbor, 7 December 1941. Rear Admiral Isaac C. Kidd, USN, and Captain Franklin Van Valkenburgh, USN, were posthumously awarded the Medal of Honor. They were both killed when the USS *Arizona* blew up from magazine explosions and a direct bomb hit on the bridge."

The Navy Department Board of Awards turned down the recommendation, however, explaining that it was "the opinion of the Board that to award the Medal of Honor posthumously in this case would establish a precedent for awards to everyone who had lost or subsequently may lose his life while at his battlestation."

"He miscalculated. Missed the turret top, and crashed to the main deck. Somehow, he was assisted in leaving the ship and making it to Ford Island." Hardy suffered multiple leg fractures and was medically discharged. Cory started following Baker, but recalled, "I got to the searchlight platform and got held up. I said, 'To hell with the traffic rules' and went down the starboard side to the quarterdeck." Seaman Harvey Milhorn climbed down from his station in the birdbath. "I went down the starboard side to the searchlight platform. At the top of the ladder lay First Lieutenant Simensen. He was in his white dress uniform. He had been hit in the stomach and his blood looked real red against the white uniform."

Baker meanwhile reached the boat deck, which "was a mass of wreckage and fire. Several men who had been killed were lying there." McCurdy and Nightingale saw

Medal of Honor Citation
Captain Franklin Van Valkenburgh, USN

"For conspicuous devotion to duty, extraordinary courage and complete disregard of his own life, during the attack on the Fleet at Pearl Harbor, T. H., by Japanese forces on 7 December 1941. As Commanding Officer of the USS *Arizona*, Captain Van Valkenburgh gallantly fought [for] his ship until the USS *Arizona* blew up from magazine explosions and a direct bomb hit on the bridge which resulted in the loss of his life."

Captain Franklin Van Valkenburgh, USN. *Naval Historical Center NH 75840*

The smoke from *Arizona* continues to billow upward, dominating the sky over battleship row. *History Division, USMC*

Arizona's aft section, with Turret No. 4 just above water level. *West Virginia* (outboard and sinking) and *Tennessee* (pumping water) moored just ahead. Ford Island is on the right. *National Archives 80-G-32424*

the same horrible sight. "The passageways were a white-hot furnace. There were charred bodies everywhere. The wounded and burned were staggering out to safety only to face death shortly because of their charred condition. Most were blind and had their clothes burned off. The quarterdeck was even worse. There were bodies of men. We'd seen this from above, but it didn't register clearly until we got down there."

McCurdy found Duveene. "My first sergeant was on the quarterdeck, burned beyond recognition. I knew him by his voice. He called us Marine champions. He yelled out for us to 'Swim for it, champions.'" Crawford also ran into him. "I found First Sergeant Duveene standing

near a ventilator shaft on the starboard side of the quarterdeck. Had I not known him so well, I would not have recognized him. His clothing was completely burned off his body. His outer skin was also burned off. I spoke with him. He told me, 'Don't try to go back inside, everything in there is all burned up. I'm not going to make it. Get the hell out of here!'" Bond was there also, "burned black, but still on his feet. He died before they could evacuate him." Aviation Machinists Mate First Class George D. Phraner fought his way out of the smoke-filled aft magazine to the deck, where he collapsed. "Behind me, a Marine lay dead on the deck, his body split in two."

Abandon Ship

Nightingale and McCurdy reached the quarterdeck but were impeded by "a man walking ahead of us with his arms outstretched because he was blind. He was in gruesome pain from burns which covered his whole body." McCurdy was horrified when he saw "one of the ship's

A fireboat pulls alongside *Arizona*; the fire would not be extinguished for two days. *History Division, USMC*

cooks, a big husky guy sitting on the deck, a man who had helped prepare the meals for the whaleboat crew. He was leaning up against a bulkhead—one of his legs had been blown off and he was just sitting there looking at the blood pumping out of the stump. Men were coming out of hatches from below decks; many naked and badly burned. We tried to help but every time we touched them, their skin came off in our hands."

The two enlisted men got split up. Nightingale "went between number three and number four turret to the starboard side with the major, where we found Lieutenant Commander Fuqua ordering the men over the side and assisting the wounded. He seemed exceptionally calm. The major stopped and they talked for a moment." Sergeant Baker also observed the commander. "I saw Lieutenant Commander Fuqua still on the quarterdeck aiding men over the lifeline and directing others who were shocked too badly to move to abandon ship; there is no doubt in my mind that many men could never have reached safety except for the superb manner in which he kept control of the situation, for there was a constant hail of splinters and the ship was being machine-gunned continuously."

At the start of the attack, Lieutenant Commander Fuqua was knocked unconscious by the bomb that struck the faceplate of Turret No. 4 . When he came to, "the ship was a mass of flames amidships on the boat deck and the deck aft was awash. The antiaircraft battery and machine guns were still firing at this time." Fuqua organized a firefighting detail, which succeeded in keeping the fires from the quarterdeck long enough to "pick up wounded that were running down the boat deck out of the flames." After finding out that he was the senior officer aboard, Fuqua ordered all hands to abandon ship. The *Arizona* could not be saved.

Medal of Honor Citation Lieutenant Commander Samuel G. Fuqua, USN

"For distinguished conduct in action, outstanding heroism, and utter disregard of his own safety above and beyond the call of duty during the attack on the Fleet in Pearl Harbor, by Japanese forces on 7 December 1941. Upon commencement of the attack, Lt. Comdr. Fuqua rushed to the quarterdeck of the USS *Arizona* to which he was attached where he was stunned and knocked down by the explosion of a large bomb which hit the quarterdeck, penetrated several decks, and started a severe fire. Upon regaining consciousness he began to direct the fighting of the fire and the rescue of wounded and injured personnel. Almost immediately there was a tremendous explosion forward, which made the ship appear to rise out of the water, shudder, and settle down by the bow rapidly. The whole forward part of the ship was enveloped in flames which were spreading rapidly, and wounded and burned men were pouring out of the ship to the quarterdeck. Despite these conditions, his harrowing experience, and severe enemy bombing and strafing, at the time, Lt. Comdr. Fuqua continued to direct the fighting of fires in order to check them while the wounded and burned could be taken from the ship and supervised the rescue of these men in such an amazingly calm and cool manner and with such excellent judgment that it inspired everyone who saw him and undoubtedly resulted in the saving of many lives. After realizing the ship could not be saved and that he was the senior surviving officer aboard, he directed it to be abandoned, but continued to remain on the quarterdeck and directed abandoning ship and rescue of personnel until satisfied that all personnel that could be had been saved, after which he left the ship with the boatload. The conduct of Lt. Comdr. Fuqua was not only in keeping with the highest tradition of the naval service but characterizes him as an outstanding leader of men."

Lieutenant Commander Samuel Glenn Fuqua, USN. *Naval Historical Center NH 92306*

Sergeant Baker ran down the officer's ladder to the quarterdeck. "The first person I saw was Lieutenant Commander Fuqua. He was very calm and aiding men over the side—these men who had been burned severely and were barely able to stand. Many apparently could not see and would not have made it without the commander. His calmness gave me courage." Fuqua ordered Baker "over the side." The Marine stripped down to his skivvies and slipped into the oil-covered waters. Halfway to Ford Island he saw Shapley and Nightingale struggling in the water; a bomb had blown them off the ship. The explosion had also stripped Shapley's clothes off.

Nightingale remembered that he had just taken off his shoes, when he suddenly found himself in the water. "When I surfaced, I couldn't use my arms and legs. I was suffering from shock. I saw my buddies hanging onto a pipeline that ran between the ship and Ford Island. They were cheering me on but I simply couldn't do it. I was scared of drowning or that a bomb might land close and kill me with concussion. I thought, 'How ridiculous! I'm young and have so much to live for.'" Just as he was foundering, Shapley swam over and grabbed him by the front of his shirt. "Put your arms on my shoulders," Shapley ordered. "Don't struggle or I'll bang you!" They struck out for shore, but had gone only a short distance before Shapley started retching with nausea from the underwater concussion. Baker was too far away to help. "I could see that the major was very tired and was risking drowning by hanging onto Nightingale." Suddenly Shapley gasped, "I'm going down, let go!" He

Silver Star Citation
Major Alan Shapley, USMC

"The President of the United States takes pleasure in presenting the Silver Star Medal to Major Alan Shapley, U.S. Marine Corps, for gallant and courageous conduct during the attack on the United States Pacific Fleet by enemy Japanese forces in Pearl Harbor, Territory of Hawaii, December 7, 1941. While swimming toward Ford Island after his ship had been bombed and set afire by the enemy, Major Shapley noticed a shipmate in distress in the water and about to go under. With no thought for his own safety, he braved the hazards of continuous enemy strafing and bombing to swim to the assistance of his helpless shipmate and, although exhausted himself, persisted in his efforts until he finally succeeded in bringing him safely ashore. His heroic action, performed at great peril to his own life, was in keeping with the highest traditions of the United States Naval Service."

Major General Clayton V. Vogel (left) presents the Silver Star to Lieutenant Colonel Alan Shapley (center) and the Navy Cross to First Lieutenant Charles T. Lamb. *History Division, USMC*

Arizona as seen from Ford Island, smoke eclipsing the view southeast toward Merry Point and the submarine base.
National Archives 80-G-32538

The *West Virginia* (outboard and listing to port) and the *Tennessee* after the attack. *US Navy 32414*

slowly slipped under the water, dragging Nightingale with him.

Shapley sank only a few feet before touching bottom. He pushed up, pulling Nightingale with him and struck out again. By this time, Nightingale had regained use of his limbs and thought he could make it alone, so he pushed Shapley away. The major thought the corporal had panicked and was struggling against his efforts. "Knock it off, Goddamit!" he snarled, grabbing Nightingale again and pulling him to safety. Nightingale was convinced that Shapley saved his life. "I would have drowned but for the major." McCurdy, too far away to help, made a promise after watching Shapley make the rescue. "If I ever have a son, he will be named Alan, after Major Alan Shapley." He kept that promise; he married a woman, appropriately named Pearl, in 1951, and they had two children, Sandra and Alan.

Seaman Musick, a navy survivor, bumped into Corporal Soley, who had gotten separated from the others and was burned. "I think he had a pair of khaki shorts on and a skivvy shirt. But his hair had been scorched and burnt like those Indians that just had this row of hair down their head. That's the way he looked to me." Both men were dazed. "We stood there for a while and kind of looked around. There were men on fire rolling around all over the deck trying to put the fire out. Soley said, 'I

Many survivors used the pipeline in the foreground to help reach Ford Island. *History Division, USMC*

guess we'd better get off this thing.' " They spotted the gangway that had been rigged between the ship and the quay. It was broken and turned up on its side, leaving only a two-foot-wide board to cross on. Somehow the two men managed to get over the shaky plank to safety.

Cory noticed the men on the gangway. "The problem was that the ship was settling and the mooring lines were getting very taut. I didn't want to make the trip across there, but I had to do something quickly. I made up my mind and started across. Suddenly one of those six-inch ropes parted and whipped past my head. It just missed me!" As he reached the quay, the plank fell into the water.

Musick spotted Platoon Sergeant Edward J. Carter in the water. "He was hollering for help, so I got down off the quay and on the pilings, and there was a piece of line

there. I threw it to him and pulled him over. The only thing that I can remember that the man had on was his sidearm. He had been standing guard on the bridge." He rejoined Soley, who told him, "We'd better get down off the quay because if those things, the mooring lines, burst or break, they'll cut you in half!" The two slipped off the edge to a boat landing where they were picked up by a rescue boat.

Cory didn't wait for a rescue boat; he dived into the water. "When I hit that cold water, I wished I had taken off my shoes because I simply could not swim with those

Oil fires on the water made escaping sinking ships that much more difficult. *National Archives 80-G-32578*

heavy brogans in the condition I was in. Then, I remembered what my father had told me about floating and I eventually made my way over to the dredge pipeline pier. During the swim, there were bomb splashes nearby; there was strafing in the water. You could feel the impact of the bullets. There was a tremendous amount of confusion and noise. Oil was bubbling up from ruptured fuel tanks and congealing on the water. It was a glob-like carpet six inches thick, which was catching fire and slowly drifting toward me."

Crawford used the mooring lines to get off the ship. "When I reached the quay, I sat down and removed my shoes before diving into the water. Almost immediately a motor whaleboat pulled alongside me and a crewman half-pulled, half-dragged me into the boat. I helped them pull other men from the water until the boat was full. The coxswain took us to Ford Island."

0854: The second wave of 170 aircraft begins their attack. Lieutenant Abe described the scene. "Antiaircraft fire was intense . . . a group of black puffs appeared to our right and then another group quite near. Every gun in the ships and on shore was firing without pause." The second wave lost six fighters and fourteen dive bombers.

Cory went looking for Young, who had made it to the island ahead of him. "I saw him retching beneath a palm tree, and I said, 'We'd better get under cover.' We went into a garage, where Young started throwing up again. We went outside underneath this tree probably in momentary confusion. He said, 'Help me get my trousers off.' They were oil soaked and burning his legs. We had just started to get them off, when a bomb

Japanese attacker headed for its target. Note black puffs of antiaircraft fire. *National Archives 80-G-32475*

exploded quite near. We were lifted up into the air and flung down on the ground again. Young got up crying in anger, his trousers up around his abdomen. 'Goddamn, Cory,' he said. 'I'm having trouble today! I can't even get my pants off!' " The two located the other Marine survivors and hunkered down in an air-raid bunker.

Crawford climbed up the bank and reached a small roadway. "I found another man, burned to a crisp, even his eyelids were peeled off. I asked him his name. He recognized my voice and said, 'My God, Crawford! Is it that bad?' It was Quincy Jones, one of my fellow Marines. I saw that he didn't have any dog tags and obviously would not live. I told a nearby navy corpsman to 'tag this man.' Jones died prior to reaching the navy hospital."

After the frantic ride from his apartment, Jack Earle's taxi finally screeched up to the main gate, where several heavily armed Marine sentries warily eyeballed a frenzied crowd of returning servicemen, many of whom wore civilian clothes. Earle remembered one navy officer had a great deal of trouble convincing the guards to let him in because of his Asian features. He was an All-American athlete at the Naval Academy, but they still weren't buying his story. Earle made his way to the Merry Point Landing. "It was a mess," he recalled. "Flames and smoke hung over battleship row. Oil covered the water—some of it on fire. *Arizona* was burning like crazy; a huge cloud of black smoke billowed skyward. *West Virginia*, next to my old ship the *Tennessee*, was burning furiously. One of the first things I saw was a Japanese aerial torpedo lying on the beach. An admiral wandered around in a daze, saying 'Ain't this a mess!' A sailor finally led him away. Many small boats nudged into the pier, calling out the names of their ship to pick up stranded shipmates. I noticed immediately that no boat came in from the *Arizona*."

While Earle was trying to find a way to Ford Island, Shapley reached the island and "was shocked to see four or five hundred men walking around all burnt, like charred steak. You could just see their eyes and mouths. It was terrible!" He rounded up the detachment survivors and got them under cover in a concrete bombproof, after which he wandered over to the housing area looking for something to wear. A navy wife he knew gave him two unlikely pieces of emergency gear—a red

scarf and a jar of Heinz pickles! "I walked to the airfield, which wasn't very bright of me, because the attack was still going on. I wanted to get a machine gun and get back in the fight." Fortunately, he ran into Chief Watertender Joe Karb, who took him in hand and gave him a change of clothes. As they walked along, Shapley related the highlights of his escape. Suddenly, a line of Japanese machine-gun bullets stitched a line of holes in the ground alongside them. The two sprinted for a low concrete wall. "Hell," Karb related, "the major—he beat me over, barefooted and all!"

Shapley, by this time, was suffering from shock. He was visibly shivering and having difficulty talking. The chief found a bottle of whiskey and gave the officer a glassful, which in his exhausted condition just about put him under. Shapley managed to make it to the Marine barracks. "I was so tired that I went to sleep on the Sunday

The USS *Shaw* explodes in the background as sailors watch from the Ford Island seaplane base. The wing of a wrecked PBY is in the foreground. *US Navy 19948*

Arizona as seen from Ford Island, with fires visible on the ship and the water. *History Division, USMC*

papers in the CO's porch and I didn't wake up until about eight or nine o'clock that night. I woke up when the shooting started. Our own planes from the *Enterprise* were shot down! The next morning I went to headquarters and found a way back to the States because I was detached from *Arizona*."

McCurdy also wandered over to the housing area. "I walked through the back door of the fenced quarters. No one was home, however. I saw oatmeal cooking on the stove, so I took it off and turned the burner off and went to Ford Island Headquarters. I remained there until Tuesday p.m. helping with the wounded and assisting at the armory with the machine-gun post on top of one of the buildings." After being relieved, McCurdy reported to the receiving station. "I saw Commander Fuqua there. He directed me to go through the clothing issue line and draw a navy work clothing sea bag. I recall I accepted everything except the white hat. I just couldn't see a Marine wearing a white hat. After a scrub down, a clean shave, and a good meal, Commander Fuqua assigned me to the *Tennessee*. I went that night with several sailors. They had written orders; I had nothing. Try to tell a chief master at arms in blackout condition that I was a Marine in navy clothing; no identification, no hat, coming aboard for duty. Needless to say, I wasn't officially signed in until a Marine Sea School classmate stationed on the

ship identified me. I was then issued a steel helmet and put on duty—you guessed it—in the crows' nest atop the main mast! My only injuries throughout the entire ordeal were slight burns to my palms from the hot railing down the ladder. My hearing was affected by the blast. My ears were ringing for several weeks and it took me many days to remove the black oil from my hair, nose, eyes, and ears."

Earle caught a boat to reach Ford Island, "which the Japanese had bombed the bejesus out of" and made his way to the closest point abreast of *Arizona*. "I found the surviving members of the detachment in a bomb shelter. They were a dazed, bedraggled-looking bunch, soaking wet, no shoes, missing parts of uniforms—and mentally exhausted." By this time the main attack was over, although "the odd Japanese plane continued to fly over." With the *Arizona* nothing but a blazing wreck, Earle thought to himself, "What the hell am I going to do with the survivors? I took them to my old ship, the *Tennessee*, which was pinned against the quay by the *West Virginia*. We walked across the fresh-water pipe that fed the battleships. My old shipmates greeted me warmly, because

Smoke from the *Arizona* (out of frame to right) fills the sky as boat crews look for survivors from the *West Virginia* (also on fire and sinking) and the USS *Tennessee. National Archives 80-G-32720*

they thought I had been killed." First Sergeant Roger M. Emmons of the *Tennessee* was thankful to see Earle again. "It was a great shock to us when we learned how many of *Arizona*'s Marines had been killed. Most of the survivors had sore guts caused by the shock of bombs exploding in the water as they swam ashore."

Pfeiffer watched the destruction of the fleet at Cinc-Pac headquarters overlooking the harbor. "About 1100 the last wave of bombers, which were high level, came over. A group of officers, some five to seven, were in the operations office looking through a louvered window at the bombers. Suddenly, there was a 'ping' as glass was broken. When we turned, we saw a dark mark on Admiral Kimmel's uniform above his heart. A tumbling bullet had come through the window and struck the admiral. My reaction was that that bullet, not only symbolically

but actually, terminated his career and active life." Pfeiffer said the staff could only watch the attack. "The emergency was too sudden and too great . . . all of Hawaii, army, navy, civilian, was in shock. The afternoon was filled with rumors of Japanese landings at various places on Oahu. The fleet operations officer rushed into my office saying, 'My God, do something, the Japanese are landing at Nanakuli!' All available men were fighting fires or preparing weapons for further attacks. At the navy yard, the Marine barracks, submarine base, and Ford Island, machine guns were mounted on roofs for antiaircraft fire."

That night, Cory was on watch when he witnessed American planes being fired on. "Everybody was trigger-happy. We shot down four of our own planes. The wildest rumors were going around. The Japs had landed on the other side of the island and were pushing across the island and we'd soon be captured; and they'd sunk all the carriers; and they hadn't gotten the *Enterprise*, and it's blown the hell out of the Jap fleet; and so on. By and large, it was a bunch of stuff you didn't believe, but you wanted to hear anyway."

Mrs. Earle's Story

"The Office of Naval Intelligence in the Alexander Young Building, where I was employed as a secretary, sent a car later that morning to gather up as many of its employees as it could. We were told to bring a toothbrush and a change of clothes as we might have to stay overnight. As it turned out, we were there at the hotel for a week, standing watches every four hours among other things. War involves a lot of paperwork!

"One morning several days after the attack, I had permission and a pass from our Navy Captain boss to go out to Pearl Harbor to meet Jack. I had not known where he was until the Chaplain of the *Tennessee* telephoned me saying, 'If you want to see someone you know, come out to the 1010 Dock at 11 a.m.' When I met Jack at the dock we had only about 10 minutes together before he had to return to the *Tennessee*, his former ship, as the *Arizona* had been destroyed and burned by the Japanese. The ship above the water line was still smoking, and Jack's face was blackened with smoke and grime blowing from the wreck . . . but he looked awfully good to me! Thank God for our fortune."

Above: Burning ships along battleship row, as seen from the Naval Station. *History Division, USMC*

Inset: Pearl Harbor after the Japanese attack. *History Division, USMC*

Salvage diver covered with oil after being below decks of the *Arizona*. *National Archives 80-G-47618*

THE AFTERMATH

"Lots and lots of bodies [floated in the harbor]—a grisly sight."
—Captain John Earle

The battleships *Oklahoma*, *Arizona*, and target ship *Utah* were sunk. Battleships *California* and *West Virginia*, and minelayer *Oglala*, were sunk but raised and returned to service. The battleships *Nevada*, *Pennsylvania*, *Tennessee*, and *Maryland*; cruisers *Raleigh*, *Honolulu*, and *Helena*; destroyers *Cassin*, *Shaw*, and *Downes*; and auxiliary ships *Curtis* and *Vestal* were damaged, but repaired.

The USS *Arizona* lost more men than any other ship in the navy, before or since. Her complement of 1,514 men suffered 1,177 dead, or 77.7 percent. Of her 337 survivors, a number of them had been on leave, liberty, or detached duty ashore, meaning that the actual loss rate of those onboard at the time of the attack was between 80 and 90 percent. *Arizona*'s loss accounted for more than half the 2,117 navy and Marine Corps fatalities in the attack. Approximately 277 bodies were recovered, leaving an estimated 900 men entombed on the ship.

The survivors stayed aboard the *Tennessee* for two weeks before being transferred to the Marine barracks for individual assignment. The Marine Detachment USS *Arizona* was officially disbanded December 19, 1941. Lamar Crawford prepared the final muster roll. "All the detachment's records, including individual Marine Service Record Books, were burned," Crawford recalled. "The only official record that was recovered a few days later was the November 1941 payroll. It survived because it was in the disbursing officer's safe, one deck below the Marine compartment, which navy divers were able to open. I used that to prepare the official and final December muster roll."

Japanese losses on December 7 were twenty-nine aircraft, fifty-five airmen, and nine midget submarine crewmen. (On December 10, the Japanese Sixth Fleet submarine *I-70*, part of the Hawaiian Operation, was attacked twice by SBD Dauntless dive bombers from the USS *Enterprise*. Damaged in the first attack, the second attack sunk her, resulting in the loss of 121 crewmen.) Commander H. L. Young, commander of the *Enterprise* Air Group, assessed the Pearl Harbor attack from a military standpoint: "The attacking planes came in down-sun, making shallow dives [about 45 to 50 degrees]. The average release height [was] about a thousand feet, although in some cases releases were made as low as three hundred to four hundred feet, indicating that their bombs were armed the instant they left the rack. After releasing, their evasive tactics were sound, keeping low and constantly changing course. My only criticism of this particular attack was that they all came in from the same direction—however, the ineffectiveness of our AA fire, lack of air opposition, and the manner in which they pressed their attacks home . . . combined to make the attack practically perfect."

Rescue and Recovery

Even during the bombing, rescue operations had swung into high gear. Small boats darted in and out of the

Author's collection

flames and smoke trying to save wounded and burned shipmates. Boatswain's Mate Second Class John Anderson, who had to evacuate his GQ station, helped load injured men into the boats that hovered around *Arizona*, until Lieutenant Commander Fuqua ordered him over the side. He reached Ford Island and appropriated an unmanned whaleboat. He and another sailor took it back to the ship, but found more dead than survivors. Two other rescuers swam to a boat near *Arizona*, cut it loose, and took it back to the crew's gangway. They climbed aboard and carried wounded shipmates until their craft was filled. On the way to the hospital ship *Solace*, they scooped men out of the water. Hundreds were rescued by the actions of men like these.

Captain Earle saw "bodies floating in the harbor and around the ship—lots and lots of bodies—a grisly sight!" Gradually, rescue of the injured turned into recovery of the dead. Earle recalled, "Initially, small boats would snare the legs and haul them in to the landing." His wife saw the same grisly sight. "I passed stretches of water busy with small boats pulling what looked like blackened logs tied together. I did not realize at first that the 'logs' were human bodies burned during the attack and float-

ing in the harbor before they were collected." After being in the water for a while, the bodies deteriorated so another method was used. A wire scoop was attached to the bow, like a streetcar bumper, which was run underneath the body. It was then lifted up and taken ashore."

The fire on the *Arizona* burned for two days, preventing recovery attempts. However, those remains on the superstructure were collected, along with those that floated to the surface. Finally, when the fire burned out, salvage drivers entered the ship to determine the extent of damage. Conditions below decks were extremely dangerous. There was no light and the drivers had to feel their way along passageways that were often bomb damaged and filled with wreckage that could trap them. They had to worry about sharp edges that could slice open their diving suits or cause serious injury. And, there remained more than nine hundred badly decomposed bodies trapped below decks. In a macabre scene, the first hard-hat diver working his way along a flooded passageway sensed something floating overhead. He carefully reached up and felt a large bag-like object. As he pushed it away, his hand sunk into the sausage. Suddenly he realized it was a body! The diver struggled to control his terror and revulsion. Every dive was the same, their movement attracted bodies that floated in their wake.

One of the divers found a cluster of dead in one of the compartments. He suggested that they could be floated to the surface through an access trunk. The result was horrifying. They were in an advanced state of decay, bloated, headless, with only bones remaining of their legs and arms. Clothes had rotted away, along with any identifying marks—dog tags were long since lost. When they surfaced in the hot tropical air, the smell was overpowering, forcing the recovering parties to wear gas masks. Even that was not enough. Many men got sick. They had to wrestle the gruesome remains into body bags—at close range. Forty-five of *Arizona's* crew were recovered before the effort was halted. The navy decided the dead were not to be disturbed and declared the ship a grave site.

Casualties

The Naval Hospital was in the flight path of the raiders. Approximately twenty Japanese planes, moving at high speed and only about one hundred feet off the ground, flew directly over the hospital buildings. They did not shoot at the hospital, but about ten minutes into the attack a flaming Japanese plane, swerving away from the main hospital building, crashed into the corner of the

At left, water is sprayed on the *Arizona*'s destroyed bow section *National Archives 80-G- 32612*

A salvage crew pulls alongside the burned-out hulk of the *Arizona. National Archives 80-G- 32608*

CPO quarters and laboratory building. The building was destroyed, and the two-man crew was killed. Their bodies were recovered from the wreckage and moved to the hospital's morgue.

As bombs rained down on Ford Island and battleship row, the staff rushed to man aid stations. Within minutes, the first wounded arrived, quickly swelling to hundreds as rescue operations swung into high gear. Soon ambulances, military and civilian trucks, personal cars and even wagons that had been pressed into service were making their way to Hospital Point. The three-hundred-bed hospital was overwhelmed. Every square yard of corridor space was lined with stretchers. The staff established a triage station, which directed the casualties, depending on

the severity of their injuries, to various treatment stations. Many of the wounded suffered flash burns, the extent of the injury depended on what they were wearing. The hospital staff commented, "A number of patients who died as a result of extensive body burns would not have died had they been wearing more clothes when injured." Others were so badly burned that nothing could be done to save them; the staff did what they could to lessen their pain. First Sergeant Duveene and Corporal Bond were among this latter group. An unknown number of lightly wounded were treated and released, and almost one thousand battle casualties were admitted before the end of the day.

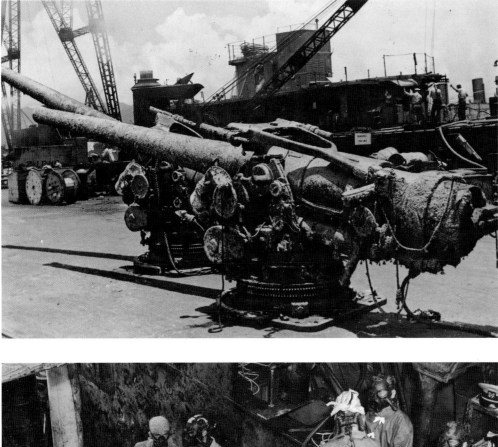

Salvaged guns of the Marine secondary battery. *National Archives 80-G-041625*

Salvage divers aboard *Arizona. National Archives 80-G-041627*

The hospital also became a gathering place for those killed in action. "Practically the entire basement of the laboratory and nurses' quarters and the ground in the immediate vicinity of these buildings were utilized as a temporary morgue. The dead were stacked like cordwood outside the door." The hospital pathologist tried to identify the remains and prepare them for burial but "identification was extremely slow, difficult, and at times impossible. Few records were available; a number [of] enlisted men [were] in clothing marked with several names; bodies were badly charred and mutilated; sometime only portions of bodies were brought in; finger-

that a larger area was needed. A new cemetery was created in the Red Hill area of Halawa, while others were buried at the Nuuanu Cemetery. The bodies were buried in trenches, with a numbered stake marking individual caskets. Chaplains officiated at funeral services each afternoon over the bodies of those buried that day. A Marine guard rendered honors with a firing party and a bugler blowing taps. At the end of World War II, the Territory of Hawaii offered the War Department the Puowaina Crater (Hill of Sacrifice), an extinct volcano, for use as a cemetery. The 116-acre National Memorial Cemetery of the Pacific, commonly known as the Punchbowl, was opened with the internment of 776 remains from the Pearl Harbor attack.

Salvage

Salvage efforts were begun even as the wounded and dead were being evacuated. The *Arizona*'s after section was relatively intact, which allowed divers to recover the crew's pay records, confidential documents, and a large amount of cash out of the disbursing officer's safe. Crawford remembered that "the navy disbursing officer on the *Arizona*, Ensign H. B. Walsh, was concerned as to whether the contents of his office safes were lost. He had more than four hundred thousand dollars cash on hand, plus blank U.S. Treasury checks, and payroll records for both navy and Marine Corps personnel inside the safes. He gave the combinations to navy salvage divers who, after

prints were often unobtainable because of absence of fingers or because they were badly damaged. The absence of metal identification discs seriously hampered this work and was responsible for the non-identification of the dead in a majority of such cases." They tried to identify the dead through billfolds, letters in pockets, inscriptions on rings—anything that might give them a clue as to the bodies' identity. It was a grisly business "trying to match up two legs, arms, a head and torso."

The dead were buried as quickly as possible in various sites on the island. The navy bought land in the Oahu Cemetery, Honolulu, but it quickly became apparent considerable trial and error, managed to get the safes open. Most of the cash and vital records were recovered intact, although some were in poor condition due to water and oil damage." A large amount of chinaware, silver from the officer's mess, and the ship's postal canceling machine were also recovered. One of the salvage divers was an *Arizona* survivor. He spent more than a hundred hours working below decks, eventually finding his own locker and retrieving his fountain pen and rosary.

The bow section was another matter entirely; the upper deck was a mass of ruptured, twisted metal, stark testimony to the force of the explosion. The mainmast tripod leaned drunkenly over the shattered bridge, which was black and distorted by fire. The armored deck and hull plates were folded back like the petals of a flower. The blast had vented through the sides, "blowing them outward almost to a horizontal position." The forecastle decks had buckled, creating a cavity that caused the forward turret to fall more than thirty feet into the hull. Its 14-inch guns

remain aboard, trained forward in the sailing position. Passageways had collapsed or were choked with debris, preventing entry into any of the forward spaces.

Divers were sent down to determine if the ship could be salvaged. They discovered a crack almost a foot wide that ran down and under the hull. *Arizona*'s back was broken. The navy decided that raising her would not be worth the effort and proceeded to strip her of useable equipment and armament. All wreckage above the water line was removed, along with much of the 14-inch ammunition. Four 5-inch 25-caliber antiaircraft guns, two main battery turrets, and other miscellaneous equipment were recovered. The ship's anchors were pulled from the mud. One of the 19,585-pound anchors is now on display at the USS *Arizona* Memorial Visitors Center at Pearl Harbor and the other in the Wesley Bolin Memorial Park in the state capital complex in Phoenix. Her turrets were turned over to the army for use as coastal defense guns. One was emplaced at Kaneohe

Arizona Battle Damage

The navy reported that the *Arizona* was struck by eight bombs; however, other studies suggest that she was hit with only four 800-kilogram weapons:

1. Port side on the antiaircraft deck.
2. Port side close to outboard so that it probably detonated in the area of the antitorpedo bulkhead.
3. Turret No. 4, which ricocheted and exploded in the captain's pantry.
4. Forward on the starboard side of Turret No. 2.

An archaeological survey in 1987 determined that the bow was nearly severed; the forward armored deck was torn and twisted. One large section was peeled back toward the port bow. Twisted and torn fragments of steel litter the decks. Turret No. 1 was intact, its three fourteen-inch guns trained forward but it has dropped twenty feet into the hull when the ship blew up. Turrets No. 3 and 4 were salvaged to be used as coastal defense guns. The ship contained one and one-half million gallons of fuel oil, which is still being released at a rate of one drop every fifteen seconds. It is said these are the "Tears of the *Arizona*."

Aft section of the *Arizona*, looking forward along battleship row.
National Archives 80-G-32609

Above: A crane begins removing *Arizona*'s foretop. *National Archives 80-G-64594*

Right: The foretop swings free of the collapsed tripod mast. *National Archives 80-G-64595*

(Mokapu Head) and designated Battery Pennsylvania. It was not until four days before Japan surrendered that the battery was considered operational.

USS Arizona Memorial

On December 1, 1942, *Arizona* was officially stricken from the register of the navy. For years afterward, the burned-out hulk quietly rusted away, forgotten except by the families of the men entombed in her hull and the occasional navy ship, which unofficially rendered honors, as if she was still commissioned. In 1950, Admiral Arthur W. Radford, commander in chief of the Pacific Fleet, established a small memorial on the rusted hulk. A flagpole was attached to the stump of a leg of the tripod and an American flag was raised and lowered daily. Seven years later, Hawaii's delegate to Congress, John Burns, proposed construction of a more suitable monument. The bill passed, with the proviso that no government funds be used. A public fund drive was launched to collect the five-hundred-thousand-dollar construction cost. It reached its goal in 1960. Elvis Presley performed at a sold-out concert in Pearl Harbor's Block Arena and donated the proceeds, sixty-five thousand dollars, to the fund.

Construction started in 1960 based on a design by Alfred Preis. The design features a bridge-like structure spanning *Arizona*'s sunken remains, without actually touching it. The memorial is 184 feet long and varies in width from 27 feet at the center to 36 feet at the ends. Its height varies from 14 feet at the center to 21 feet at the ends. The memorial is divided into three sections: a museum room; an assembly area that can accommodate two hundred people for ceremonies; and a shrine room

The Pearl Harbor memorial dedicated to the Marine Detachment, November 2005. *Author's collection*

that contains a marble wall listing the names of *Arizona*'s 1,177 crewmen killed in the attack, with the Marines listed together at the end. The flagstaff is mounted on a portion of the battleship's superstructure and does not touch any portion of the memorial itself.[1]

Marine Detachment Memorial

On November 14, 2005, the Commandant of the Marine Corps, General Michael W. Hagee, dedicated a memorial to *Arizona*'s Marine detachment. It is located on a point of land between the USS *Arizona* Memorial Visitors Center and the USS *Bowfin* Submarine Memorial and Park. The memorial consists of a thirty-six-foot flagpole embedded in a seven-sided concrete base on which seven bronze plaques, inscribed with the names of the detachment, are fixed. The plaques are three feet tall and weigh 185 pounds.

One hundred and nine Marines made the ultimate sacrifice during the attack on Pearl Harbor. The *Arizona* suffered seventy-three of those fatalities, 67 percent of the total. Only fifteen of her eighty-eight man detachment survived December 7, 1941. According to the final muster, the bodies of sixteen *Arizona* Marines were identified and buried at Red Hill Cemetery. These bodies were later exhumed and reburied at the National Memorial Cemetery of the Pacific. The remains of five additional Marines from the *Arizona* were identified after the completion of the final muster. Fifty-two Marines remain entombed in the *Arizona*.

APPENDIX A
Muster Roll of
Marine Detachment Arizona,
December 1941

MUSTER ROLL OF OFFICERS AND ENLISTED MEN OF THE U. S. MARINE CORPS

MARINE DETACHMENT, U.S.S. ARIZONA, MB, NYd, Pearl Harbor, T.H.

From **1 December,** to **31 December**, 19 41, inclusive

RECAPITULATION

	GENERAL OFFICERS	COLONELS	LIEUTENANT COLONELS	MAJORS	CAPTAINS	FIRST LIEUTENANTS	SECOND LIEUTENANTS	AVIATION CADETS	CHIEF WARRANT OFFICERS	WARRANT OFFICERS	ENLISTED MEN							TOTAL
											FIRST GRADE	SECOND GRADE	THIRD GRADE	FOURTH GRADE	FIFTH GRADE	SIXTH GRADE	SEVENTH GRADE	
REGULAR MARINE CORPS																		
Attached at beginning of period.			1	1		1	1				1	1	1	4	11	38	20	80
Joined.					1												1	2
Total attached.			1	1	1	1	1				1	1	1	4	11	38	21	82
Detached and transferred.				1	1	1						1	1	2	6	1		14
Deserted.																		
Dis. Missing in Action.			1			1					1	1		3	9	32	20	68
Discharged.																		
Resigned and dismissed.																		
Retired and transferred to Reserve.																		
Total separated.			1	1	1	1	1				1	1	1	4	11	38	21	82
Attached at end of period.																		0
DETACHED AND AWAITING RETIREMENT																		
At home awaiting retirement.																		
Retired.																		
MARINE CORPS RESERVE																		
Attached at beginning of period.																6		6
Joined.																		
Total attached.																6		6
Detached and transferred.																1		1
Deserted.																		
Dis. Missing in Action.																5		5
Discharged.																		
Resigned and dismissed.																		
Retired and transferred to inactive status.																		
Total separated.																6		6
Attached at end of period.																		0
GENERAL COURT-MARTIAL PRISONERS																		
Attached at end of period.																		
TEMPORARILY ATTACHED																		
During period.																		
OTHER ARMS OF THE SERVICE																		
Navy, attached at end of period.																		
Army, attached at end of period.																		

NOTES:
1-4, At Sea, Hawaiian Operating Area.
5-6, At Pearl Harbor, T.H.
7, Attacked by Japanese Dive Bombers and torpedo planes at approximately 7:55 a.m., at Pearl Harbor, T.H. Ship blown up by explosion of forward magazines, burned, and began sinking at approximately 8:13 a.m. Abandoned ship at approximately 8:15 a.m. Missing action, 73. Survivors distributed as follows:
7-17, Temp det d MD, USS TENNESSEE.
18-31, Temp det d MD, USS OKLAHOMA.
31, Organization disbanded at 12:00 midnight, auth MarCorps radio #262159, December, 1941.

History Division, USMC

NO.	NAME AND RANK	ENLISTED	REMARKS	1192
		DETACHED		
	MAJOR			
1	SHAPLEY, Alan.		1-5, Co, MD; Legal Aide to CO; Baseball O; 6, detached, awtg transportation to 2d MarDiv, FMF, MCB, San Diego Calif.; 7, participated in action resultant of surprise attack by Japanese Air Forces on NYd, Pearl Harbor, T.H.; 8, emb and 10 sailed fr Pearl Harbor, T.H., via USS NEOSHO. Auth 15 das delay in reporting upon arr US.	
	CAPTAIN			
1	EARLE, John H., Jr.	✓	6, jdfr MD, USS TENNESSEE, at Pearl Harbor, T.H.; 6 only, CO, MD; Legal Aide to CO; 7, participated in action resultant of surprise attack by Japanese Air Forces on NYd, Pearl Harbor, T.H.; 7, emb on board USS TENNESSEE, at Pearl Harbor, T.H., auth verbal orders ComBatFor; 7-17, temp det d MD, USS TENNESSEE; 18-disemb at Pearl Harbor, T.H., and assigned to temp det d Co "A", MB, NYd, Pearl Harbor, T.H., auth orders Fleet Pooling Officer; 18-31, temp det d Co "A", MB, NYd, Pearl Harbor, T.H., awtg final disposition MD; 31, at 12:00 midnight, to MB, NYd, Pearl Harbor, T.H.	
		TRANSFERRED		
	PLATOON SERGEANT			
1	CARTER, Edward J.	✓	7, participated in action resultant of surprise attack by Japanese Air Forces on NYd, Pearl Harbor, T.H.; 8 only, temp det d MB, NYd, Pearl Harbor, T.H.; 9-31, temp det d MD, USS OKLAHOMA, awtg final disposition MD; 31, at 12:00 midnight, to MB, NYd, Pearl Harbor, T.H.	
	SERGEANT			
1	BAKER, John MacR.	✓	1-6, SGDP(p)2cl; See Footnote "A".
	CORPORALS			
1	NIGHTINGALE, Earl C.	✓	See Footnote "A".
2	SOLEY, Michael.	✓	See Footnote "A".
	PRIVATES, FIRST CLASS			
1	BRAHAM, Edward J.	✓	1-6, SGDP(ss)2cl; See Footnote "A".
2	CABINESS, Frank R.	✓	See Footnote "A".
3	CORY, James E.	✓	1-6, SGDP(p)1cl; See Footnote "A".
4	CRAWFORD, Lamar S.	✓	Det. Clk; 1-6, SGDP(t)2cl; See Footnote "A".
5	GOODMAN, Kenneth D.	✓	7, participated in action resultant of surprise attack by Japanese Air Forces on NYd, Pearl Harbor, T.H.; 8 only, temp det d MB, NYd, Pearl Harbor, T.H.; 9-31, temp det d MD, USS OKLAHOMA,

(DO NOT WRITE BELOW THIS LINE)

History Division, USMC

First document (top left)

MUSTER ROLL OF OFFICERS AND ENLISTED MEN OF THE U.S. MARINE CORPS
MARINE DETACHMENT, U.S.S. ARIZONA, MB, NYd, Pearl Harbor, T.H.
FROM 1 December, TO 31 December, 1941, INCLUSIVE

NO.	NAME AND RANK	ENLISTED	REMARKS
			awtg final disposition MD: 31, at 12:00 midnight, to MB, NYd, Pearl Harbor, T.H.
6	YOUNG, Donald G. PRIVATE		See Footnote "A".
1	HARDY, Charles L.		7, wounded in action resultant of surprise attack by Japanese Air Forces on NYd, Pearl Harbor, T.H.; 7-17, sk USNH, NYd, Pearl Harbor, T.H.; 18, to MB, NYd, Mare Island, Calif, as patient USNH, NYd, Mare Island, Calif?
	MISSING IN ACTION		
	LIEUTENANT COLONEL		
1	FOX, Daniel R.		1-6, Div Mar O, Div One, BatShips, BatFor, U.S. Pacific Fleet; JA-Court of Inquiry; See Footnote "B"
	SECOND LIEUTENANT		
1	SIMENSEN, Carleton E.		1-6, Det O; Basketball O; See Footnote "B"
	MASTER GUNNERY SERGEANT		
1	HOLZWORTH, Walter.		See Footnote "B".
	FIRST SERGEANT		
1	DUVEENE, John.		See Footnote "B".
	SERGEANTS		
1	BARAGA, Joseph.		1-6, SGC2cl; See Footnote "B".
2	OLE, Charles M.		1-6, SGC2cl; See Footnote "B".
3	FINCHER, Dexter W.		1-6, SGC2cl; See Footnote "B".
	CORPORALS		
1	BARTLETT, David W.		See Footnote "B".
2	BOND, Burnis L.		See Footnote "B".
3	BORUSKY, Edwin C.		See Footnote "B".
4	DE LONG, Frederick E.		See Footnote "B".
5	JERRISON, Donald D.		See Footnote "B".
6	MC CARRENS, James F.		1-6, SGDP(t)2cl; See Footnote "B".
7	PIASECKI, Alexander L.		1-6, SGC2cl; See Footnote "B".
	FIELD COOK		
1	SMILINICH, Stanley S.		See Footnote "B".
	FIELD MUSIC CORPORAL		
1	SHIFF, Jack B.		See Footnote "B".
	PRIVATES FIRST CLASS		
1	BAILEY, George R.		See Footnote "B".
2	BELT, Everett R., Jr.		See Footnote "B".
3	DREESBACH, Herbert A.		See Footnote "B".
4	DURIO, Russell.		See Footnote "B".
5	ERSKINE, Robert W.		See Footnote "B".
6	FILES, Woodrow W.		See Footnote "B".
7	FLEETWOOD, Donald E.		See Footnote "B".
8	GRIFFIN, Lawrence J.		See Footnote "B".
9	HARMON, William D.		See Footnote "B".
10	HUDNALL, Robert C.		See Footnote "B".
11	HULTMAN, Donald S.		See Footnote "B".
12	HUX, Leslie C.		See Footnote "B".
13	JONES, Quincy E.		See Footnote "B".
14	KRAHN, James A.		1-6, Msm; See Footnote "B".
15	LINDSAY, James E.		See Footnote "B".
16	LOVSHIN, William J.		See Footnote "B".
17	MINEAR, Richard L., Jr.		See Footnote "B".
18	MOSTEK, Francis C.		See Footnote "B".
19	MOLATUBBY, Henry G.		See Footnote "B".
20	O'BRIEN, Joseph B.		See Footnote "B".
21	PATTERSON, Clarence R., Jr.		See Footnote "B".
22	POWELL, Jack S.		See Footnote "B".
23	SCHNEIDER, William J.		See Footnote "B".
24	SCOTT, Crawford E.		See Footnote "B".
25	SCOTT, George H.		See Footnote "B".
26	SHIVE, Gordon E.		See Footnote "B".
27	STEVENSON, Frank J.		See Footnote "B".
28	STOVALL, Richard P.		1-6, Msm; See Footnote "B".

FEB 23 1942   Sheet No. 2

Second document (right)

O.	NAME AND RANK	ENLISTED	REMARKS
29	WEBB, Carl E.		See Footnote "B"; 1-6, SGP(s)1cl.
30	WHISLER, Gilbert H.		See Footnote "B".
4	WINDLE, Robert E.		See Footnote "B".
	ASSISTANT COOK		
1	FINCHER, Allen B.		See Footnote "B".
	PRIVATES		
1	AMUNDSON, Leo DeV.	16Jul41	6, ldfr Co "A", MB, NYd, Pearl Harbor, T.H.; See Footnote "B".
2	ATCHISON, John C.		See Footnote "B".
3	BEATON, Freddie.		See Footnote "B".
4	BLACK, James T.		See Footnote "B".
5	BRICKLEY, Eugene.		See Footnote "B".
6	CHANDLER, Donald R.		See Footnote "B".
7	DAVIS, Virgil D.		See Footnote "B".
8	DAWSON, James B.		See Footnote "B".
9	EVANS, David D.		1-6, Msm; See Footnote "B".
10	FITZGERALD, Kent B.		See Footnote "B".
11	HERRICK, Paul E.		See Footnote "B".
12	HOPE, Harold W.		See Footnote "B".
13	HUFF, Robert G.		See Footnote "B".
14	KEEL, Billy M.		See Footnote "B".
15	PEDROTTI, Francis J.		See Footnote "B".
16	POWER, Abner F.		See Footnote "B".
17	REINHOLD, Rudolph H.		See Footnote "B".
18	WEIER, Bernard A.		See Footnote "B".
19	WINDISH, Robert J.		See Footnote "B".
20	WITTENBERG, Russell D.		See Footnote "B".
	MARINE CORPS RESERVE		
	TRANSFERRED		
	CLASS III(a)		
	PRIVATE		
1	MC CURDY, Russell J.		7, participated in action resultant of surprise attack by Japanese Air Forces on NYd, Pearl Harbor, T.H.; 8 only, temp d NAS, Pearl Harbor, T.H. 9-17, temp d MD, USS TENNESSEE; 18-31 temp d MD, USS OKLAHOMA, awtg final disposition MD; 31, at 12:00 midnight to MB, NYd, Pearl Harbor, T.H.
	MISSING IN ACTION		
	CLASS III(a)		
	PRIVATES		
1	DUNHAM, Robert W.		See Footnote "B".
2	HUGHES, Marvin A.		See Footnote "B".
3	KALINOWSKI, Henry.		1-6, Msm; See Footnote "B".
4	SZABO, Theodore S.		See Footnote "B".
	FIELD MUSIC		
1	HAMEL, Don E.		See Footnote "B".

FOOTNOTES
"A"   7, participated in action resultant of surprise attack by Japanese Air Forces on NYd, Pearl Harbor, T.H.; 7, emb on board USS TENNESSEE, at Pearl Harbor, T.H., auth verbal orders ComBatFor; 7-17, temp d MD, USS TENNESSEE; 18, disemb at Pearl Harbor T.H., and assigned to temp d MD, USS OKLAHOMA, auth orders Fleet Pooling Officer; 18-31, temp d MD, USS OKLAHOMA, awtg final disposition MD; 31, at 12:00 midnight, to MB, NYd, Pearl Harbor, T.H.

"B"   Missing in action since approximately 8:00 a.m., 7 December, 1941.

John H. Earle
JOHN H. EARLE, Jr.
Captain, U.S. Marine Corps,
Commanding Detachment.

FOOTNOTES
(Ltr, CG, DF, 17Mar42.)
Pvt Hardy, Charles L.   (TRANS)   *** 18, emb and 19, sailed fr Honolulu, T.H., via SS PRES COOLIDGE.

Forwarded from MB, NYd, Pearl Harbor, T.H., 5 January, 1942.

(WRITE NOTHING BELOW THIS LINE)

Third document (bottom left)

(WRITE NOTHING ABOVE THIS LINE)

MUSTER ROLL OF OFFICERS AND ENLISTED MEN OF THE U. S. MARINE CORPS
MARINE DETACHMENT, U.S.S. ARIZONA, MB, NYD, PEARL HARBOR, T.H.
FROM 1 December, TO 31 December, 1941, INCLUSIVE

NO.	NAME AND RANK	ENLISTED	REMARKS
			FOOTNOTES, continued.
	KILLED IN ACTION		
2dLt	Simensen, Carleton E.		*** See footnote "C". Grave number unknown.
MGySgt	Holzworth, Walter		See footnote "C". Grave #272.
1stSgt	Duveene, John		See footnote "C". Grave #138.
Corp	Bond, Burnis L.		See footnote "C". Grave #145.
Corp	Jerrison, Donald D.		See footnote "C". Grave #518.
PFC	Bailey, George R.		See footnote "C". Grave #403.
PFC	Jones, Quincy E.		See footnote "C". Grave #137.
PFC	Lindsay, James E.		See footnote "C". Grave #515.
PFC	Shive, Gordon E.		See footnote "C". Grave #517.
PFC	Stevenson, Frank J.		See footnote "C". Grave #509.
PFC	Stovall, Richard P.		See footnote "C". Grave #301.
PFC	Webb, Carl E.		See footnote "C". Grave #364.
PFC	Whisler, Gilbert H.		See footnote "C". Grave #519.
Pvt	Dawson, James B.		See footnote "C". Grave #140.
Pvt	Weir, Bernard A.		See footnote "C". Grave #521.
Pvt	Wittenberg, Russell D.		See footnote "C". Grave #512.
			FOOTNOTE "C": 7, at about 8:00 a.m., killed in action on board USS ARIZONA, while engaged in repulsing Japanese Air Attack at Pearl Harbor, T.H. GO 20 does not apply. Remains interred at Red Hill Cemetery, Oahu, T.H.

APPENDIX B
Lieutenant General T. Holcomb, CMC Letter to Simensen Family

IN REPLYING ADDRESS
MAJOR GENERAL COMMANDANT
AND REFER TO NO.

06679-2
AHC-85-efc

FOR DEFENSE
BUY
UNITED
STATES
SAVINGS
BONDS
AND STAMPS

HEADQUARTERS U. S. MARINE CORPS
WASHINGTON

JUL 3 1 1942

My dear Mr. Simensen:

I have the honor to transmit to you herewith a letter of commendation posthumously awarded by the Secretary of the Navy to your son, the late Second Lieutenant Carleton E. Simensen, United States Marine Corps, citing him for heroic action in battle on the occasion of the Japanese attack on the U. S. Pacific Fleet at Pearl Harbor on December 7, 1941.

I take this occasion, as Commandant of the Corps which he so splendidly served, to add my own commendation of his heroism and devotion to duty.

Words, written or spoken, are futile on an occasion such as this, but I earnestly hope that the Department's recognition of your son's gallantry may somewhat alleviate the sorrow of Mrs. Simensen and yourself in the irreparable loss you have sustained.

Sincerely yours,

T. HOLCOMB
Lieutenant General U.S.M.C.,
The Commandant U.S. Marine Corps.

Enclosure.

Mr. C. O. Simensen,
703 Fifth Street,
Devils Lake, North Dakota.

Elwyn B. Robinson Department of Special Collections, Chester Fritz Library, University of North Dakota

APPENDIX C
Lamar Crawford Affidavit and Casualty Roster

VOL 3781 PAGE 318

96-R0012006

STATE OF TEXAS :
COUNTY OF SMITH :

Filed for Record in:
SMITH COUNTY, TEXAS
MARY MORRIS - COUNTY CLERK
On Apr 08 1996
At 10:07am
Deputy - Jennette Steveson

AFFIDAVIT

BEFORE ME, the undersigned authority, on this day personally appeared LAMAR S. CRAWFORD, a resident of the aforesaid State and County, who swore on oath that the following facts are true:

1. "My name is Lamar Smead Crawford. I am the same Lamar Smead Crawford who enlisted in the United States Marine Corps at New Orleans, Louisiana on June 14, 1940, and was later assigned to serve with the U.S. Marine Detachment on board the Navy Battleship U.S.S. ARIZONA. I reported on board the U.S.S. Arizona at Pearl Harbor, T.H. September 18, 1940, and served continuously with Division 7 (the U.S. Marine Detachment) through and including the disbandment of that unit at Pearl Harbor December 31, 1941.

2. As a part of my assigned duties while a member of the Marine Detachment, U.S.S. Arizona, I assisted the 1st Sergeant, John Duveene, and another Marine Clerk in the handling of Administrative work such as preparation of Muster Rolls, Payrolls, and general correspondence for that unit. I was one of 13 on-board Marine Survivors incident to the bombing and sinking of the Arizona by hostile (Japanese) forces at Pearl Harbor on December 7, 1941.

3. A copy of the November, 1941 payroll for the Marine Detachment (prepared by me) was the only official document relating to the Administrative Records of the Marine Detachment recovered by Navy divers from the burned out, sunken ship following the disaster. As the only surviving member of the 1st Sergeant's office staff, I subsequently reconstructed sufficient data for the preparation of closing Muster Rolls, Payrolls, and settlement of accounts for those members of the Detachment living and dead during the period 8-31 December, 1941. A listing of the entire membership of that Detachment (as of 7 December, 1941) is attached.

Lamar Smead Crawford
Lamar S. Crawford, Marine Corps Service No. 285619"

Subscribed and Sworn to before me by the said Lamar S. Crawford this 8th day of April, 1996, to certify which, witness my hand and seal of office..

Joan A. Hayes
NOTARY PUBLIC, STATE OF TEXAS

JOAN A. HAYES
NOTARY PUBLIC
STATE OF TEXAS
My Commission Expires 8-26-99

VOL 3781 PAGE 319

Page 1 of 2

MARINE DETACHMENT, U.S.S. ARIZONA
CASUALTIES
7 Decmember, 1941

NAMES	RANK	HOME OF RECORD
AMUNDSON, Leo Devere	Pvt.	LaCrosse, Wisc.
ATCHISON, John Calvin	Pvt.	St. Louis, Mo.
BAILEY, George Richmond	PFC.	Santa Monica, Ca.
BARAGA, Joseph	Sgt.	Channing, Mich.
BARTLETT, David William	Corp.	Bell, Ca.
BEATON, Freddie	Pvt.	Chickasha, Ok.
BELT, Everett Ray, Jr.	PFC.	Kirkwood, Mo.
BLACK, James Theron	Pvt.	Covin, Ala.
BOND, Burnis Leroy	Corp.	Wiggins, Miss.
BORUSKY, Edwin Charles	Corp.	Langdon, N.Dak.
BRICKLEY, Eugene	Pvt.	Uniondale, Ind.
CHANDLER, Donald Ross	Pvt.	Millport, Ala.
COLE, Charles Warren	Sgt.	Arlington, Wash.
DAVIS, Virgil Denton	Pvt.	Alton, Mo.
DAWSON, James Berley	Pvt.	Louisville, Ky.
DE LONG, Frederick Eugene	Corp.	Cridersville, Ohio
DREESBACH, Herbert Allen	Pvt.	Chicago, Ill.
DUNNAM, Robert Wesley	Pvt.	Houston, Tx.
DURIO, Russell John	PFC.	Sunset, La.
DUVEENE, John	1stSgt.	Los Angeles, Ca.
ERSKINE, Robert Charles	PFC.	Siloam Springs, Ark.
EVANS, David Delton	Pvt.	New Orleans, La.
FINCHER, Allen Bradley	AsstCook	Canton, Tx.
FINCHER, Dexter Wilson	Sgt.	Prinville, Ore.
FINLEY, Woodrow Wilson	PFC.	Selmer, Tenn.
FITZGERALD, Kent Blake	Pvt.	Salt Lake City, Utah
FLEETWOOD, Donald Eugene	PFC.	North Ft.Dodge, Iowa
FOX, Daniel Russell	Lt.Col.	Long Beach, Ca.
GRIFFIN, Lawrence John	PFC.	Westwego, La.
HAMEL, Don Edgar	FieldMusic	Chicago, Ill.
HARMON, William Daniel	PFC.	Portland, Ore.
HERRICK, Paul Edward	Pvt.	Kenosha, Wisc.
HOLZWORTH, Walter	MGySgt.	Bergenfield, N.J.
HOPE, Harold Wyatt	Pvt.	Borger, Tx.
HUDNALL, Robert Chilton	PFC.	Pittsburgh, Tx.
HUFF, Robert Glenn	Pvt.	Ft. Worth, Tx.
HUGHES, Marvin Austin	Pvt.	Houston, Tx.
HULTMAN, Donald Standly	PFC.	Dassel, Minn.
HUX, Leslie Creade	PFC.	Dodson, La.
JERRISON, Donald Dearborn	Corp.	Des Moines, Iowa
JONES, Quincy Eugene	PFC.	Perry, Fla.
KALINOWSKI, Henry	Pvt.	Ashtabula, Ohio
KEEN, Billy Mack	Pvt.	Newark, Tx.
KRAHN, James Albert	PFC.	Langdon, N.Dak.
LINDSAY, James Ernest	PFC.	Montrose, Ca.
LOVSHIN, William Joseph	PFC.	Ely, Minn.
MCCARRENS, James Francis	Corp.	Ottawa, Ill.
MINEAR, Richard John, Jr.	PFC.	Phoenix, Ariz.

VOL 3781 PAGE 320

Page 2 of 2. Casualties, Marine Detachment, U.S.S. Arizona - Cont'd

MOSTEK, Francis Clayton	PFC.	Dover, Idaho
NOLATUBBY, Henry Ellis	PFC.	Bakersfield, Ca.
O'BRIEN, Joseph Bernard	PFC.	Chicago, Ill.
PATTERSON, Clarence Rankin,Jr.	PFC.	Long Beach, Ca.
PEDROTTI, Francis James	Pvt.	St. Louis, Mo.
PIASECKI, Alexander Louis	Corp.	Acme, Wyo.
POWELL, Jack Speed	PFC.	Los Angeles, Ca.
POWER, Abner Franklin	Pvt.	Clinton, Okla
REINHOLD, Rudolph Herbert	Pvt.	Salt Lake City, Utah
SCHNEIDER, William Jacob	PFC.	Chicago, Ill.
SCOTT, Crawford Edward	PFC.	N. Kansas City, Mo.
SCOTT, George Harrison	PFC.	Spokane, Wash.
SHIVE, Gordon Eshom	PFC.	Laguna Beach, Ca.
SIMENSEN, Carleton Elliott	2ndLt.	Devils Lake, N.Dak.
SNIFF, Jack Bertrand	FieldMus.Corp.	Speer, Ill.
STEVENSON, Frank Jake	PFC.	Manhattan, Kan.
STOVALL, Richard Patt	PFC.	Hartley, Tx.
SWIONTEK, Stanley Stephen	FldCook	Chicago, Ill.
SZABO, Theodore Stephen	Pvt.	Castalia, Iowa
WEBB, Carl Edward	PFC.	Waco, Tx.
WEIR, Bernard Arthur	Pvt.	Downers Grove, Ill.
WHISLER, Gilbert Henry	PFC.	Bloomfield, Iowa
WINDISH, Robert James	Pvt.	St. Louis, Mo.
WINDLE, Robert England	PFC.	Jacksonville, Ill.
WITTENBERG, Russell Duane	Pvt.	Darwin, Minn.

SURVIVORS - U.S. MARINE DETACHMENT - U.S.S. ARIZONA

NAMES	RANK (as of 7Dec41)	REMARKS
BAKER, John MacRae	Sgt.	Survived war - now deceased
BRAHAM, Edward James	PFC.	
CABINESS, Frank R.	PFC.	* Survived War - lives Ark.
CARTER, Edward J.	P1Sgt.	
CORY, James Evans	PFC.	Survived War - now deceased
COURSEY, John Paul	1stLt.	Survived War - lived Ga.1984
CRAWFORD, Lamar Smead	PFC.	* Survived War - lives Texas
EARLE, John H., Jr.	Capt.	Survived War - lives Hawaii
GOODMAN, Kenneth Dale	PFC.	
HARDY, Charles L.	Pvt.	(broke leg on board - Med.Disch).
MC CURDY, Russell J.	Pvt.	* Survived War - lives Ind.
NIGHTINGALE, Earl C.	Corp.	Survived War - now deceased
SHAPLEY, Alan	Major	Survived War - now deceased
SOLEY, Michael	Corp.	Survived War - Died 6/99
YOUNG, Donald George	PFC.	Survived War - now deceased

NOTE: * Only 3 of on-board survivors currently living -(Feb.1996).
Capt. John H. Earle, Jr., and 1stLt. John P. Coursey were on authorized weekend leave (on Oahu) 7Dec41.

CERTIFICATION: I, Lamar Smead Crawford, former Marine Detachment Clerk, prepared the above listing from official Marine Corps Records reconstructed by me at Pearl Harbor, T.H. during the period December 8-31, 1941 and other official Navy Historical Data.

Lamar Smead Crawford

APPENDIX D
Captain Franklin Van Valkenburgh Letter to Diane Gillette

Capt. Franklin Van Valkenburgh, U.S.N.
U.S.S. Arizona

November 24th 1941.

My dear Diane :-

You and I have a date, and I think I told you it should be next Sunday. Now I find we are not going to be here next Sunday. Can we change it to Sunday, December 7th.

I thought it might be fun, if you, and your friends would come out to the ship at 3.00 o'clock and have a chance to go around the ship first before dinner, then we will have dinner in the cabin here, and then see the movies on the quarter deck afterward.

Were you able to find six friends who were interested.? Six other young ladies, or 3 girls and 3 boys?

If it suits you I will come in in my gig and meet you at the officers club landing @ three o'clock sharp, on Sunday, December 7th.

Cordially
Franklin Van Valkenburgh

U.S. Army Museum, Fort DeRussy, Hawaii

APPENDIX E
Profiles

James Cory

Cory was promoted to corporal soon after Pearl Harbor. He served in the Pacific theater during the remainder of the war and took part in the occupation of Japan. He mustered out of the Marine Corps in 1945 and attended Southern Methodist University under the GI Bill. Not finishing college, he married and raised a family. His first postwar job was selling insurance, but he spent most of his days as building director at a Neiman-Marcus department store. He died on July 9, 1978, at age fifty-six.

James Cory, July 1977. *Lamar Crawford*

John Coursey

After the attack, Coursey was assigned to the Marine barracks, where he served as a guard company commander until October 1942. He volunteered for flight training and was sent back to the United States for primary training at Dallas, Texas. In January 1943, Coursey went on to Pensacola, where he received his wings, and then on to Jacksonville for operational scout-bombing training. Upon completion of his training and carrier qualifications, he was assigned instructional duty at Cecil Field, Florida. In September 1944, he was ordered overseas for duty with the First Marine Air Wing, as commanding officer of VMR-152, a transport squadron. His unit supported operations in the Philippines, Solomon Islands, Okinawa, and the Palaus. After the war, Coursey served in a variety of aviation assignments in the United States before receiving orders to Korea, as executive officer of Marine Air Group 33. He returned to the United States in April 1953 for duty at the U.S. Air Force Air University. Coursey was promoted to brigadier general in August 1962.

Major John Coursey.
History Division, USMC

Lamar Crawford

Crawford returned to the States in November 1942 and remained until 1943. He was promoted to warrant officer and ordered overseas with the 3rd Marine Airwing. Before shipping out, he married his high school sweetheart. After the Japanese surrender, he returned to the United States and was discharged on January 11, 1946. He joined the U.S. Postal Service and retired after thirty-six years. His son served in Vietnam as a Marine. Crawford is eighty-four years old and is one of two *Arizona* survivors.

Pfc. Lamar Crawford, March 1942. *Lamar Crawford*

Jack Earle

Jack Earle was born January 7, 1915, in Reading, Pennsylvania. After graduating from high school, Jack attended the Virginia Military Institute, receiving a commission as a second lieutenant in 1936. While attending the officers' training school in Philadelphia, he married Barbara Ferry, who was attending Drexel College. Barbara was the only married graduating student. The two started their married life at the Marine Barracks, Quantico. Like all young officers, it

Jack Earle.

was difficult to make ends meet. Their first "quarters" was a one-room hovel above a five-and-dime; Barbara remembers the neon sign shining in the window throughout the night, and they shared a bathroom with several other newly married couples. Following an assignment on the West Coast, Earle joined the USS *Tennessee* and then *Arizona*. Eleven months after Pearl Harbor, the couple departed Hawaii aboard a military transport, zigzagging all the way to the West Coast. They drove cross-country to Pensacola, where Earle attended flight school. After receiving his wings, he was ordered to Jacksonville for operational training in dive bombers (SBDs). In 1944, Earle reported to Marine Air Group 24 (MAG-24) on Bougainville, Solomon Islands. A short time later, the MAG shipped out for the Philippines, where they came under control of General Douglas MacArthur. Jack was indignant because press releases never identified them as Marines, only as MacArthur's dive bombers. After the war, the Earles were transferred on average every two to three years—Washington, D.C., Brooklyn, California, Hawaii, Virginia, and an exotic tour at the Imperial Defense College, London, England. In the meantime, their family had grown to include three boys and two girls.

Russell McCurdy

In 1944, McCurdy was commissioned and ordered overseas. He participated in the landing on Peleliu and Okinawa, and the occupation of North China at the end of the war. He was classified as a "sole surviving son," when his only brother was killed in Europe. He served in Korea during the war and retired as a lieutenant colonel in 1965. After retirement he worked in retail sales for fifteen years. Russell McCurdy passed away in 2005.

Russell John McCurdy (left), Pearl McCurdy, and Lamar Crawford, 1977. *Lamar Crawford*

Earl Nightingale

After leaving the Marine Corps, Nightingale went on to a career in radio as an actor, commentator, and executive. He became widely known for playing the titular character in *Sky King,* a radio-drama series about a former military pilot who patrolled the skies around his Flying Crown Ranch in his Cessna. He later had a daily commentary program that was broadcast worldwide.

Alan Shapley

Shapley was born February 9, 1903, in New York City. As a young boy, he attended many different schools because his father was a career naval officer, who was frequently transferred to meet the needs of the service. In 1927, he graduated from the U.S. Naval Academy with a commission as a Marine second lieutenant. He served in a variety of posts and stations commensurate with his rank throughout the 1930s. In June 1940, he was assigned to the USS *Arizona*. During World War II, he commanded the 2nd Raider Battalion and later the 2nd Raider Regiment in the fighting on Bougainville. He took command of the 4th Marine Regiment upon the dissolution of the Raiders and led it through the Emirau, Guam, and Okinawa campaigns. For heroism on Guam, he was awarded the Navy Cross, the second highest American decoration for bravery, and a Legion of Merit for Oki-

Major General Alan Shapley, USMC.
History Division, USMC

nawa. After the war, he served in a succession of staff assignments in Washington, D.C., and San Diego. In 1953, Shapley went to war again, serving as the chief of staff, 1st Marine Division, and as the senior advisor to the Korean Marine Corps. Returning home in 1955, he served first as assistant division commander, 1st

Marine Division, and later as commanding general, 3rd Marine Division. His last assignment, commanding general Fleet Marine Force Pacific, was at Camp H. M. Smith, Hawaii. He retired in 1962. Lieutenant General Alan Shapley died on May 12, 1973, at the National Naval Medical Center, Bethesda, Maryland.

Carleton Simensen

Edwin Rupp, who played football with Simensen, met him in Pearl Harbor before the war. "We bunked together . . . and went on liberty several times. On the Sunday prior to December 7th, we and two others drove around the island in an old Model T. Carleton was well liked and was a very good Marine officer." Another friend described Simensen as "a great individual, widely respected, everybody liked him." His sister wrote, "When the telegram came telling us of his death our thoughts went immediately to the beautiful girl, Verona, whom he planned to marry on his first leave from Hawaii. When my mother opened the trunk that was sent to us after his death, it was filled with things for Verona and their future married life."

Second Lieutenant Carleton Elliott Simensen (center) on a recruiting tour at the University of North Dakota, 1940. Second Lieutenant Virgil Banning is on the left, and Second Lieutenant Orville Bergman is on the right.
Elwyn B. Robinson Department of Special Collections, Chester Fritz Library, University of North Dakota

Notes

Prologue
1. Gordon W. Prange, *December 7, 1941: The Day the Japanese Attacked Pearl Harbor*. New York: McGraw-Hill, 1988, p. 106.
2. Prange, *December 7, 1941*. p. 164.
3. Gordon W. Prange, *God's Samurai, Lead Pilot at Pearl Harbor*. Washington, DC: Brassey's, 1990.

Chapter 2
1. Robert Debs Heinl, *Soldiers of the Sea*. Annapolis: United States Naval Institute, 1962, pp. 15, 16.
2. Heinl, *Soldiers of the Sea*. p. 95.
3. Terry Munderloh, "USS *Arizona*: The Vessel and the Vassal Who Christened Her." Internet: Sharlot Hall Museum, 2003.
4. Charles R. Smith, *Marines in the Revolution: A History of the Continental Marines in the American Revolution 1775–1783*. Washington, DC: History and Museums Division, U.S. Marine Corps, 1975. p. 384

Epilogue
1. Richard A. Wisniewski, *Pearl Harbor and the USS Arizona Memorial: A Pictorial History*. Honolulu: Pacific Basin Enterprises, 1986.

Bibliography

Books

Annual Report of the Navy Department for the Fiscal Year 1914. Washington, DC: GPO, 194, 1915.

Goldstein, Gordon M. and Katherine V. Dillon. *The Pearl Harbor Papers: Inside the Japanese Plans*. Washington, DC: Brassey's, 1993.

Jasper, Joy Waldron, James P. Delgado, and Jim Adams. *The USS* Arizona: *The Ship, the Men, the Pearl Harbor Attack, and the Symbol That Aroused America*. New York: St. Martin's Press, 2001.

LaForte, Robert S. and Ronald E. Marcello. *Remembering Pearl Harbor: Eyewitness Accounts by U.S. Military Men and Women*. Wilmington: S.R. Books, 1991.

Letcher, John Seymour. *One Marine's Story*. Verona, Virginia: McClure Press, 1970.

Metcalf, Clyde H. *A History of the United States Marine Corps*. New York: G. P. Putnam's Sons, 1939.

Nalty, Bernard C. *The U.S. Marines in the War with Spain*. Marine Corps Historical Reference Series, HQMC G-3, September 1958.

Prange, Gordon W. *At Dawn We Slept*. New York: Viking, 1991.

———*God's Samurai, Lead Pilot at Pearl Harbor*. Washington: Brassey's, 1990.

Prange, Gordon W., Donald M. Goldstein, and Katherine V. Dillon. *Dec. 7, 1941: The Day the Japanese Attacked Pearl Harbor*. New York: McGraw-Hill, 1988.

Richardson, James O. *On the Treadmill to Pearl Harbor: The Memoirs of Admiral James O. Richardson USN (retired)*. Washington, DC: Naval History Division, Department of the Navy, 1973.

Slackman, Michael. *Target Pearl Harbor*. Honolulu: University of Hawaii Press and Arizona Memorial Museum Press, 1990.

Smith, Charles R. *Marines in the Revolution: A History of the Continental Marines in the American Revolution 1775–1783*. Washington, DC: History and Museums Division, U.S. Marine Corps, 1975.

Stillwell, Paul. *Battleship* Arizona: *An Illustrated History*. Annapolis: Naval Institute Press, 1991.

Thomason, John W. *And a Few Marines*. New York: Charles Scribner's Sons, 1945.

Wisniewski, Richard A. *Pearl Harbor and the USS* Arizona *Memorial: A Pictorial History*. Honolulu: Pacific Basin Enterprises, 1986.

Oral History

Allen, Chester R., 1973

Brown, Wilburt S., 1967

Cushman, Robert E., 1984

Krulak, Victor H., 1973

Pfeiffer, Omar T., 1974

Personal Interviews

Crawford, Lamar

Earle, John H.

Orr, Art

Index

Abe, Squadron Leader Lieutenant Zenji, 73, 102

Akagi, 63–67, 71

Allen, First Lieutenant Chester, 10, 22

Amundson, Private Leo DeVere, 70, 84

Arizona Memorial Visitors Center at Pearl Harbor, 115, 117

Bailey, Private First Class George Richmond, 72, 82, 92

Baker, Sergeant John M., 14, 84, 87, 93, 94, 97, 98

Bond, Corporal Burnis Leroy, 20, 21, 84, 90, 96, 112

Bonhomme Richard, 25, 26

Bowfin Submarine Memorial and Park, 117

Boxer Rebellion, 29

Brooklyn Navy Yard, 29, 35

Brown, Lieutenant Wilburt S. "Bigfoot," 16, 51

California, 75, 109

Cassin, 109

Chikuma, 63

CincPac, 7, 80, 106

Congressional Pearl Harbor Investigation Committee, 51

Constitution, 31

Cory, Private First Class James E., 16, 20, 71, 82, 84, 87, 89–91, 93, 94, 101–103, 106, 123

Coursey, First Lieutenant John P., 16, 21, 73, 123

Crawford, Private First Class Lamar, 7, 70, 72, 76, 84, 85, 87, 92, 93, 94, 96, 102, 103, 109, 114, 121, 123

Curtis, 16, 109

Downes, 109

Duveene, First Sergeant John, 11–13, 16, 73, 84, 96, 112

Earle, Barbara, 71, 80, 82, 107, 110, 123, 124

Earle, Captain John H. "Jack," 9, 13, 16, 18, 21, 22, 59, 69–71, 80, 82, 103–107, 109, 110, 123, 124

Enterprise, 6, 74, 105, 106, 109

Essex, 27

Fox, Colonel Daniel "Danny" R., 70, 71, 82, 92, 94

Fuchida, Commander Mitsuo, 6, 61, 62, 74, 89

Fuqua, Lieutenant Commander Samuel G., 6, 97, 98, 105, 110

Genda, Commander Minoru, 61, 62, 71

George Washington, 40, 41

Germantown, 31

Hardy, Private Lawrence, 87, 93, 94

Hawaiian Operating Area, 48

Hawaiian Operation, 60, 109

Helena, 76, 109

Here Comes the Navy, 48

Hiei, 63

HMS Serapis, 25, 26

Holcomb, Lieutenant General Thomas, 94, 120

Holzworth, Master Gunnery Sergeant Walter, 16, 18, 20, 25, 73, 84

Honolulu, 109

Hoover, President Herbert, 29, 44–48

Hunt, Governor W. P., 31, 32

Jones, John Paul, 25, 26

Jutland, Battle of, 18

Kalinowski, Private Henry, 9–14, 16, 18, 38, 84

Kidd, Rear Admiral Isaac Campbell, 57, 70, 72, 82, 92, 94

Kimmel, Admiral Husband E., 56–59, 63, 69, 106

Krulak, Lieutenant General Victor, 18, 22

Letcher, Captain John Seymour, 18, 21, 22

Maine, 28–30

Marine Detachment Memorial, 117

Marine Sea School, 9, 105

Maryland, 109

McCurdy, Private Russell J., 13, 57, 72, 78, 87, 89, 90, 93, 94, 96, 97, 100, 105, 124

McDonald, Captain John D., 35, 38

Merry Point Boat Landing, 9, 10, 53, 99, 103

Misissippi, 20

Monroe Doctrine, 28

Musick, Seaman, 100, 101

Myers, Captain John Twiggs "Handsome Jack," 28, 29

Nagato, 59, 62, 74

Nagumo, Admiral Chuichi, 61–63, 65, 66

National Memorial Cemetery of the Pacific, 114, 117

Naval Hospital, 110–114

Nevada, 6, 7, 10, 22, 57, 75, 78, 109

New York, 23

New York Navy Yard, 29, 30

Nightingale, Corporal Earl C., 6, 7, 78, 84, 85, 87, 89, 93, 94, 96–98, 100, 124

Nimitz, Admiral, 27

Nuuanu Cemetery, 114

Oahu Cemetery, 114

Oglala, 76, 109

Oklahoma, 18, 21, 54, 87, 109, 112

Panama Canal, 28, 42, 44, 48

Paris Peace Conference, 41

Pearl Harbor Marine Barracks, 13

Pearl Harbor Navy Yard, 6, 7, 55

Pearl Harbor Submarine Base, Ford Island, 7, 9–11, 53–56, 58, 76, 78, 80, 82, 87, 91, 94, 96, 98, 99, 101, 102, 104–106, 110, 111

Pennsylvania, 16, 24, 51, 56–58, 78, 84, 109

Pfeiffer, Colonel Omar T., 57, 69, 70, 82, 106

Puowaina Crater (Hill of Sacrifice), 114

Raleigh, 109

Ramsey, Lieutenant Commander Logan, 6, 7

Red Hill Cemetery, 114, 117

Revolutionary War, 26

Richardson, Admiral James O., 49, 51, 56

Rochester, 28

Roosevelt, President Franklin D., 31, 40, 51, 59

Roosevelt, President Theodore, 28

Ross, Esther, 31, 34, 35

Sakamaki, Ensign Kazuo, 60, 63

San Francisco, 13

Shapley, Major Alan, 6, 7, 13–16, 20, 70, 71, 73, 74, 78, 84, 87, 92, 93, 98–100, 104, 105, 124, 125

Shaw, 79, 104, 109

Simensen, Second Lieutenant Carleton Elliott "Sim," 16, 73, 76, 77, 84, 85, 87, 94, 120, 125

Solace, 110

Soley, Corporal Michael, 71, 72, 74, 75, 78, 87, 93, 100, 101

Spanish-American War, 28, 29

Tennessee, 69, 70, 77, 82, 85, 96, 100, 103, 105–107, 109, 112, 124

Thomason, Colonel John W., 26, 28

Tripoli, 28

Tun Tavern, 25

U.S. Naval Academy, 57, 58

Utah, 44, 54, 109

Van Valkenburgh, Captain Franklin, 57, 70, 71, 77, 82, 91, 92, 94, 95, 122

Vestal, 89, 109

Walsh, Ensign H. B., 114, 115

Ward, 73

Wesley Bolin Memorial Park, 115

West Virginia, 69, 80, 85, 89, 96, 100, 103, 105, 106, 109, 112

White, Captain Chevey S., 69, 70, 77, 78

Wilson, President Woodrow, 39, 41

World War I, 18, 53, 70

Yamamoto, Admiral Isoroku, 51, 53, 57, 59–61, 63, 74

Yoshikawa, Ensign Takeo, 59, 62

Young, Private First Class Donald G., 87, 102, 103

Zaikaku, 63

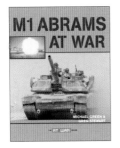

M1 Abrams At War
ISBN 0-7603-2153-1

B-17 At War
ISBN 0-7603-2522-7

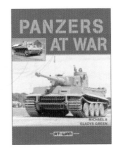

Panzers At War
ISBN 0-7603-2152-3

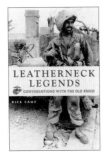

Leatherneck Legends: Coversation
with the Old Breed
ISBN 0-7603-2157-4

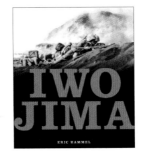

Iwo Jima
Portraits of a Battle: United States
Marines at War in the Pacific
ISBN 0-7603-2520-0

USMC
ISBN 0-7603-2532-4